IN YOUR HANDS

Good Business Strategies for Small Business Owners

TOMEKA PRESCOTT

I want you to rock your market. Give it a little shake.

Published by:

Prescott Wireless 1

817 D. West BoBo Newsome Hwy.

Hartsville, SC 29550

www.tomekaprescott.com

Printed in the United States of America
First Printing, October 2014 Edition 1

ISBN 978-0-692-26817-9 (Paperback)

Scripture taken from the New King James Version®. Copyright © 1982 by Thomas Nelson. Used by permission. All rights reserved.

Disclaimers: You must not rely on the information in the book as an alternative to legal, financial, taxation, or accountancy advice from an appropriately qualified professional. If you have any specific questions about any legal, financial, taxation, or accountancy matter you should consult an appropriately qualified professional. This report is based on personal experiences and observations of the author and is intended for educational and informational purposes only. The author and publisher have made every effort to ensure the information in the book was correct at press time. The author and publisher do not assume and hereby disclaim any liability to any party for any loss, damage, or disruption caused by errors or omissions, whether such errors or omissions result from negligence, accident, or any other cause. The reader assumes all responsibility for the use of information in this report.

Dedication

A Special Friend
God Bless You

Contents

Foreword

I would like to take this time to say how blessed I am to have met Tomeka Prescott.

Hello everyone, my name is Antionette Richardson, and I have been a mentor, but more importantly, what I think is a true friend to Tomeka Prescott since 2009 when we worked together at a mutual University. We met while in training together; I reached out to her to keep in touch through email; she responded, and the rest has been history in the making.

Since this time, Tomeka and I have communicated through busy days, nights, and in between our personal lives to make sure one or the other is "A-Okay!" I will be 49 this year, and I have to admit I have really relied on Tomeka's keen ear for listening, along with her sincere advice, wisdom, and knowledge.

Yes, at some point we think we have heard it all, seen it all, done it all, and know it all, but let me tell you something – until you ask Tomeka her thoughts and reasoning behind how to handle a

business scenario, you might want to rethink your process. She will deliver!

Tomeka has a passion for not just her students, but people in general. She currently owns a small retail business and is blessed to not have too much competition, but should it arise, in my opinion and confidence in her, she will outthink the competitor with her innovativeness, skills, abilities, and undeniable customer service.

The next time you think about running a business, think about a person who will address structure, fundamentals, and provide an explanation in a thorough but succinct way as to why business is so important to the society in which we live today. That would be Tomeka Prescott!

In closing, after reading *IN YOUR HANDS: Good Business Strategies for Small Business Owners*, you too will witness as Paul in Philippians 2:13, [13] for it is God who works in you both to will and to do for *His* good pleasure (NKJV)." This book will be a bestseller and a book that you will continue to use as a reference point when you need guidance in business. This book is a must read! It's your time!

Sincerely,

Antionette Dee Richardson, MAHR, MAHRDV, MAOM

Introduction

CONNECT. SHARE. SERVE.

How can you help others? You can do this by sharing knowledge. *IN YOUR HANDS* is a book filled with good business strategies for small business owners. If your response is thank you, my response is you are welcome!

In this book you will find business strategies to help grow your small business. You will learn about business success strategies that include: learning how to stay focused upon your own business; creating a plan when you are already in business to grow your business; funding your business; how to listen to your customers and know what they need and want; the value of practicing altruism; the benefits of offering quality products and services; adding value to your small business; the power of

branding your name and your small business name and how to do it through creative planning; creating effective back-up plans to avoid business failure; how to watch and monitor your bottom line; the importance of controlling inventory; and knowing when it's best to hire employees and outsource departments. Last, you will learn how to stay true to your own business by carrying out your mission and vision to inspire others.

I wrote this book because I want to see you grow your small business. I want to encourage you to do your best while you are in business and to always look for ways to add business growth.

The information in this book is what I have learned through experience over the past 20 years growing up working at my family's business and owning and operating a retail store.

Most importantly, I wrote this book because I want to give you a lift so you can see that you can start growing your small business wherever you live. Also, I want you to know that you can use the resources you currently have to grow your small business.

Not only do I want to give you a lift, but we can both lift each other through sharing our knowledge.

What will you find inside each chapter?

Strategies and tips to take action right now to grow your small business, motivational quotes, and real-life inspiring personal stories from when I learned that life goes on to the market in São Paulo, Brazil, when I learned that you have to be different to grow your business.

I have included real-life examples of how to add business growth, and I have included activities to help you get started on your journey to growing your business.

As you are reading this book I want you to take notes of your ideas and thoughts. I want you to create a journal. You can use a spiral notebook or a three-ring binder. Write on the outside of your journal, notebook, or three-ring binder: *IN YOUR HANDS: Good Business Strategies for Small Business Owners,* or whatever title you wish. Whatever works best for you is what counts the most. I want to start this book out by sharing a challenge with you that I had to overcome.

One major challenge I faced in life was being diagnosed with hyperthyroidism and hypothyroidism.

Hyperthyroidism is a condition of an overactive thyroid gland and hypothyroidism is a condition of an underactive thyroid gland.

Two blows one after another, during the second semester of my freshman year in college. In Chapter 1, you will find out what I didn't do.

Enjoy the journey!

Tomeka Prescott

SECTION ONE

Stay Focused
and
Grow Your Business Slowly

STAY FOCUSED
AND DON'T STOP

I NEVER GAVE UP

Who says you have to fly or even soar? You can walk it out at your own pace, as long as you are making progress.

TOMEKA PRESCOTT

I continued studying business in college, while playing sports, and working in the family business. While I may have faced a challenge, I learned that staying focused on the goals you want to achieve in life are important, and that you must push through and not give up because...

> *In three words I can sum up everything*
> *I've learned about life: it goes on.*

ROBERT FROST

LIFE GOES ON

If life gets tough, don't give up. Just as life goes on, if you face challenges when growing your small business, don't give up because business goes on too.

Every second counts.

WHAT IS STAYING FOCUSED ABOUT?

This chapter is about learning how to stay focused on growing your business. A business needs time to grow, so do not jump ahead of yourself.

In this chapter you will learn why staying focused on your business is important and how to stay focused in practical steps.

In this chapter you will learn to never take your eyes off the ball (your business), never stop growing your business, and to be ready for opportunities because everyone doesn't always get a second chance at the same opportunity.

You will answer a few questions, brainstorm a bit, and make a list to help prepare yourself to become a more focused small business owner. At the end of this chapter you will write your "FOCUS" statement paragraph. I wrote my focus statement at the end of this chapter.

THESE ARE 3 REASONS WHY STAYING FOCUSED IS IMPORTANT

YOU WANT TO BECOME A SUCCESSFUL SMALL BUSINESS OWNER

First, staying focused is important because you want to become a successful small business owner who is able to add value to your life and other people's lives as well. When operating a business, there may be a lot of things going on around you but the key is to stay focused on how you plan to grow your business.

When you focus on your small business, you are able to strengthen and build your business so you can take it to the next level. How far and wide do you plan to grow? Will you use the success strategy of staying focused to help you? The choice is yours.

YOU WANT TO GROW EACH PART OF YOUR BUSINESS

Second, when you are growing your business you want to ensure you stay focused and grow each part of your business. This includes: the customer service department, the management department, the sales department, the marketing and advertising departments. In addition to growing departments, you also want to stay focused on improving in areas that you see need improvement.

For example; if there is a need to improve your marketing strategy, focus on improving your marketing strategy. As a sole owner of a small business, you may have to improve these areas all by yourself if you decide not to outsource department tasks.

You Want to Accomplish Your Dreams in Life

Third, what's your dream? It has always been a dream of mine to continue to grow my business so I can continue to help others.

I know how exciting it is to accomplish dreams because I have accomplished several. I focused on the dreams that I had the knowledge and skills to accomplish. Some of these dreams seemed close while others seemed so far away.

The fun part is what's going on during the journey to your destination. One of my biggest dreams I have accomplished was becoming a business professor. As I look back at the steps I had to take, for example graduating from high school, college, and then graduate school, to get to where I am now, it is priceless. But to achieve my goals I had to stay focused. Another dream that I have always had was to write and publish a book. I am writing that book now. Oh yes, and the book has been published. You are reading it now. Staying focused on your dreams by taking the practical steps you need to accomplish those dreams will help make your dreams become a reality. Don't forget to reward yourself once you have worked hard to make a dream come true.

You Can Reward Yourself!

Rewarding myself continues to help me reach my goals in life. I love buying and reading new books, going to the beach, shopping, and simply having some "me" time. This keeps me energized and focused so I can take on the next challenge. I can recall being rewarded all throughout life. When I did well on a test in grade school, I was rewarded with a sticker. When I

graduated from college, I received a car. Thanks Dad and Mom. Now I am an adult so it's time to reward myself.

I understand the value of rewarding yourself when you have accomplished any goal you have had. Have you rewarded yourself before?

If yes, good job!

If, no, think of some things you like and how you plan to reward yourself when you accomplish your next goal.

I want you to remember that in business you want to take your business to the next level, improve areas of your business that need improvement, and turn your dreams into reality.

You can start by staying focused.

You can focus on doing one thing at a time when growing your small business. Since you know the importance of staying focused, now, let's learn how to do this.

HOW TO STAY FOCUSED

NEVER TAKE YOUR EYES OFF THE BALL—YOUR BUSINESS!

During my younger years, I loved to play softball. One concept I have learned from all of my coaches was to "never take my eyes off the ball." As a little girl, I followed what my coaches told me to do but never realized that I would use this same concept later in life when operating a business.

As a business owner, it is very important for you to stay focused and never take your eyes off the "ball" and when you start something, don't "stop." When you are working on growing

your business, if there are any roadblocks, I want you to have a plan in place to overcome the roadblocks to push forward.

NAIL THAT BALL—YOUR BUSINESS!

I want you to think of your small business as a "softball" and imagine you are playing the sport. Your name is called… and you are next up to bat. You are now focused. As you walk to the home plate, you keep your eyes on the ball. As the pitcher releases the ball, your eyes are still on the ball. You then nail the ball and it goes flying far out and lands not in the infield, not in the outfield, but over the gates. A home run was hit because you never took your eyes off the ball. You were determined and focused, you already knew what you wanted to accomplish before you even stepped up to the plate. Now I want you to write down the top five reasons on why it is important for you to stay focused in business and write down the top five reasons why it is important to never give up in business.

YOUR 5 REASONS TO STAY FOCUSED IN BUSINESS

1.

2.

3.

4.

5.

YOUR 5 REASONS TO NEVER GIVE UP IN BUSINESS

1.

2.

3.

4.

5.

Here are my five reasons to stay focused in business and my five reasons why it is important to never give up. Review your reasons and examine my reasons. Do we have anything in common? Let's see!

MY 5 REASONS TO STAY FOCUSED IN BUSINESS

1. To continue to grow my business so I can help make the world a better place.
2. To benefit my local community.
3. To be an inspiration to others.
4. To help others create a future.
5. It's exciting to see a business grow.

MY 5 REASONS TO NEVER GIVE UP IN BUSINESS

1. I was called to be a business owner.
2. I like to help others.
3. Being creative in business is fun.
4. I am not a quitter.
5. It's my passion.

Knowing why you need to stay focused will help you grow your business.

DON'T STOP GROWING YOUR BUSINESS

I want you to focus on growing your business every day. Open doors for yourself and others. Go for it! What do you have to lose?

TOMEKA PRESCOTT

Even if you are moving slowly, that's okay in my book; I want you to keep going. It is very hard to grow a business if you start growing your business then stop growing your business. Then start up again. If you have to crawl, keep moving. Sometimes as a small business owner, when something doesn't work out the way we would have liked it to, we may have a hard time moving on.

If you are already where you want to be as a small business owner, you may think that there is no more room for business growth. There is nothing wrong with growing to reach your maximum potential. I want you to pick up the rocks and knock down the walls and never give up on growing your business. If you start then stop, you may miss out on an opportunity to grow your business.

I keep moving by not looking in the past or trying to take a peek into the future. I take one day at a time and focus on tasks I need to complete in the present. I keep things moving by not looking

at the whole picture. When I break larger tasks into smaller tasks and go at my own pace I am able to make progress.

Now that you know to keep moving, I want you to…

FOCUS ON MOVING THESE THREE AREAS IN BUSINESS

The three areas are: growing your customer database, providing great customer service by treating your customers with respect, and always thinking of ways you can innovate new products and services to offer your customers. In the coming chapters we will discuss more about these three areas in detail so you can learn how to implement these strategies in your small business. Next, I will show you how to prepare for opportunities.

ALWAYS BE PREPARED FOR OPPORTUNITIES

You may never know when a good opportunity may come by, but as a small business owner, you have to be ready to take advantage of these opportunities. Sometimes opportunities may show up when you don't expect them to; that's why it is important to be prepared.

When I am prepared for opportunities, I have the self-confidence to follow through to do the best that I can.

I am going to show you how to prepare yourself for opportunities. However, you have to be willing to take action and know if the opportunities will help you grow your business.

When opportunities to grow my small business come my way, I ask myself these three questions because I want to give my best.

1. Can I fit the opportunity into my schedule without overextending myself?
2. How much money and time is involved with pursuing the opportunity?
3. How would the opportunity help me grow my business?

DON'T OVEREXTEND YOURSELF

First, I want you to ask yourself if you can fit this into your schedule without overextending yourself. As a small business owner, you'll want to avoid a "burnout." Remember you can't be everybody; you are YOU. Only you know how much you can handle. I can recall a burnout I want to share with you.

This burnout happened around the holiday time during one of the busiest seasons of the year - Christmas. I had to take on so many different roles, such as a buyer, Santa's little helper, a sales representative, a party organizer, and a delivery person. Now in business during the holiday seasons is when I plan to scale back on new projects so I can stay focused in business to help more customers during this busy season.

What I do to avoid burnouts?

I have chosen to delegate tasks to avoid burnouts.

When you realize what a burnout is and how to avoid it, you can continue to be productive in business by not overextending yourself. That's why I wrote this book using strategies and tips you can implement on a daily basis, weekly basis, monthly basis, or yearly basis. I want you to focus on the information that is

relevant to you and I want you to know that you don't have to apply each of these strategies or tips all at one time.

NOW LET'S PONDER THESE QUESTIONS.

Question #1

Have you experienced a burnout?

Question #2

What are some strategies and tips you used to help you overcome the burnout?

Question #3

Do you have any friends who have experienced a burnout?

Question #4

What did they do to overcome their burnout?

Question #5

How can you move on from a burnout?

Let's make a list here. You can use this space to answer these questions. Go for it!

Answer to Question # 1 _____

Answer to Question # 2 _____

Answer to Question # 3 _____

Answer to Question # 4 _____

Answer to Question # 5 _____

Now that you have answered the five questions let's keep it moving.

This Is What I Want You to Know:

THERE IS NO SUCH THING AS A FREE LUNCH

Second, I want you to know how much money and time is involved with pursuing the opportunity. I learned in Economics class in college that there is no such thing as a free lunch. When I learned about this concept, I applied it to different areas of my life. So when I receive opportunities I know that there is a cost somewhere. It's up to me to know if I am able to take on the opportunity or pass it up. Keep track of your opportunities as they come by recording them here.

OPPORTUNITY COST

Opportunity 1

Opportunity 2

Opportunity 3

Opportunity 4

Opportunity 5

Cost 1

Cost 2

Cost 3

Cost 4

Cost 5

OPPORTUNITIES COME AND GO

Focus on preparing yourself for opportunities. You never know when you will receive an opportunity to help push you forward; so be ready.

TOMEKA PRESCOTT

In business, one opportunity I received was to be interviewed by a freelancer writing a business related article. This was a once-in-a-lifetime opportunity and I knew it. I responded to the inquiry quickly, exchanged a few emails with the freelancer, and later nailed the interview. A few weeks later, I was cited in an article that went live online. I was able to think fast, and then prepare myself for this opportunity.

If you want to read articles I am cited in, you can find them here:

www.TomekaPrescott.com

As opportunities arise while you are in business, I want you to check to see if each opportunity is a good fit. Do a little brainstorming and go from there! If you decide not to act on the opportunity, stay calm and keep growing your business. Opportunities come and go. If you decide the opportunity is a good fit, accept the opportunity and do the best that you can do to shine bright.

TACKLE OPPORTUNITIES

Third, if you decide to tackle the opportunity, how would you use it to grow your business, whether it's publicity, a job offer, or a new product or service you can offer to your customers and clients?

Now let's say you have decided to tackle the opportunity. What are your next steps from here? Let's ponder upon how the outcome of the opportunity may help you grow your business.

In business, most of the opportunities I come across are the ones that allow me to offer better services and products to my customers at a lower price. When I notice price drops in the industry I work in, I work on passing this down to my customers as soon as possible.

My customers love it when I offer quality products and services at good prices below the amount they are currently paying for the same product and/or service.

An opportunity like this one usually presents itself several times throughout the year, but I have to have my eyes open to find them and a plan to carry out the opportunity. When I decide to take on opportunities, it benefits my business and my customers as well.

Also, planning will help you prepare for opportunities. We will discuss more about planning in Chapter 2.

SUMMARY

As a small business owner you want to stay focused, so don't forget to never take your eyes off the ball. Prepare yourself for opportunities: remember that you are YOU, and decide how

you'll use opportunities to help grow your small business. If you decide to tackle opportunities do the best you can do. In addition, don't give up on growing your small business.

When you give up you will never know what you could've accomplished.

AFTER READING THIS CHAPTER, IF YOU DO NOTHING ELSE I WANT YOU TO...

➢ Write a paragraph of how you plan to stay focused on the "ball" which is your "business."
➢ Write the words FOCUS at the top of the paper; take some tape and hang it on the wall near your desk.

I want you to make your focus statement visible so you can read it throughout the day.

If you need help creating your focus statement, I'd love to help you. You can contact me at:

www.TomekaPrescott.com

Okay, here I go.

FOCUS

I plan to stay focused on looking for opportunities that will continue to help me grow my small business. In addition, I plan

to stay focused on growing my business slowly because there is no need to rush business growth.

- I want to enjoy the experience.
- I want to make the journey amazing.
- I want to create something new.

If I need to knock down walls, I will knock them down. If I need to build walls, I will build them. I have the desire, determination, and dedication to win in business.

This is my focus statement. This is what I will refer back to as I continue to grow my small business.

It's time for a celebration; you have read Chapter 1! I'm going to grab a cup of coffee. Now that you are focused and you know not to stop, let's move on to Chapter 2 where you'll learn about the heart of your small business.

SECTION TWO

Business Basics – Planning and Finance

YOUR BUSINESS PLAN IS THE HEART OF YOUR BUSINESS

The lights were shining bright, they were hot, I had on my opening number dress; it was white, covered with rhinestones, and gold glitter sequences from the top and down. The bottom was all white stringy feathers. I had on four-inch heels that made me 6 foot 2 ½ inches tall. The countdown began. It was time for me to put my right foot forward and walk my walk in the opening number in a beauty pageant.

Yes, I am a pageant girl.

Since I was a baby, I've always competed in beauty pageants. I have won some and have lost some. But the key here is that I

have always had a plan. My plan was to win them all, but sometimes I fell short. Each time, I'd get back up, do a little shoulder bounce and body shake, and keep moving.

After my shake, I'd craft a new strategy for the next pageant. While competing in beauty pageants I didn't have a complicated plan, nor did I pretend to be like others. I went with the plan to be myself because that's all I can really be--I made the plan right for me.

WHY IS A BUSINESS PLAN THE HEART OF A BUSINESS?

This chapter is about creating an effective business strategy that you can use right now to add business growth.

If you don't get your business strategy right the first time, that's okay, nobody's perfect. A sports team coach may not always have a winning strategy to win every game; however, through practice a coach will learn how to revamp a strategy. It's the same in business. Small business owners learn how to revamp business strategies to stay current in the market.

Let's learn why a business plan is the heart of a business.

THE HEART OF A BUSINESS

The business plan is the heart of a small business because a plan provides a guide to follow. Having a guide to follow may help you reach your goals quicker, so always write your plans on paper.

MAKE YOUR BUSINESS PLAN RIGHT FOR YOUR SMALL BUSINESS

If you confuse yourself it can be a bit contagious;
you may end up confusing others.

TOMEKA PRESCOTT

In business, make the business plan right for your small business. A small business does not have to have an extravagant, complex business plan. For several years, I have studied and created business plans, and what I have noticed is that all business plans do not have the same parts; therefore, every business plan will not generate the same results.

I had to learn that you have to know your industry and you have to create a plan that works best for your small business. What may work for your business may not work for the same type of business in the same town. Since I know this, I knew that I had to be creative and create my own business strategy and plan for my small business.

While there are several parts to a business plan, in this chapter I am going to focus on one part of the business plan that I believe is very important. What part of the business plan do you think it is? Continue to read; I will share what I believe is one of the most important parts of a business plan.

Now answer this question.

HOW COULD YOU GROW YOUR SMALL BUSINESS WITHOUT A BUSINESS STRATEGY?

I believe the most important part of a business plan is your BUSINESS STRATEGY.

As a small business owner, you should focus on crafting your business strategy. Since you now know the business strategy is an important part of your business plan, think about how you are going to craft your strategy to add business growth to your small business.

Also, since you're now focused, put all of your energy in creating the best strategy for your small business.

PONDER THESE THREE QUESTIONS.

Question #1

Do you think all small business owners have a business plan with a well-crafted strategy?

Question #2

Do you have a well-crafted business strategy?

Question #3

How can you create a well-crafted business strategy?

These are all good questions to think about when growing your small business by implementing a business strategy.

What do you think about these questions?

HAVE A WELL-CRAFTED STRATEGY

Some small business owners may have a strategy and some may not have a strategy. All small business owners should have a well-crafted strategy. Don't shift from day-to-day, not knowing if you are growing your business. If you don't have a well-crafted strategy in place, don't worry about that. That's something you can work on.

DON'T WAIT TO START CRAFTING A WINNING STRATEGY

Envision that you are a sports coach of a basketball team. One of your main goals would be to craft a winning strategy before every game, with the ultimate strategy of winning the championship game. A coach would not wait to start crafting a winning strategy during the season. A coach would work on crafting a strategy during pre-season, during the season, and post season. Simply put, a coach will work hard to craft a strategy during all of the seasons, even during the off-season so they can see what works and does not work, then make the changes going forward.

Creating a winning business strategy works the same way. It should be an ongoing task for small business owners.

CREATE A FUTURE RIGHT NOW

Small business owners can't predict the future, but having a well-crafted strategy in a business plan, then putting that strategy to

work, and working it daily, can help create an attainable future for your business.

A future of operating a thriving business.

A future of growing the business more easily.

A future of reaching business goals.

I DON'T KNOW HOW?

These are some things to look at when crafting your small business strategy. It does not have to be complicated; a business strategy can be revamped at any time.

Practice mastering the SWOT analysis concept.

A BUSINESS STRATEGY DOES NOT HAVE TO BE COMPLICATED

Since we know that a business strategy does not have to be complicated, I am going to show you how to get started with crafting a business strategy in practical steps.

TOMEKA PRESCOTT

Implementing a business strategy will help grow your business. This is how you can get from point A to B to C.

- Know your mission and vision in business.
- Know what products and services you will sell to your customers.

- Know your market (where you will sell your products and services).

MISSION AND VISION

I know my mission. I am in business because I want to change the world to help make it a better place to live. Knowing why you are in business is important. Why are you in business? Take your time when writing this statement.

What's your mission? Write it here.

-
-
-

If you already have a mission statement that's good. You are doing big things!

I know my vision. I see my business being the backbone to my community projects. Where do you see your business going?

A vision statement is a very important statement. I like using the words "very important"; when you see these words pay close attention so nothing is missed. You can use the focus strategies in Chapter 1 to help you right now. Take your time when writing this statement. Make this statement as clear as possible.

What's your vision? Write it here.

-
-
-

How do you plan to use your mission and vision to help you create a business plan for growth?

In business, you need to know what products and services you will sell. In business, I sell cellular phones, accessories, and cell phone related services to my customers.

Know your market.

My market is the town where my business is located and the community where I live.

Do you plan to market your business to consumers in the town where your business is located? In the state where your business is located? In the country your business is located? In other countries?

You can start selling products and services to people who you know first and to consumers who live in the town where your business is located. This may consist of selling to family members and friends, too. Once you grow your business in one market, then you can venture out to sell your products and services to other markets. To get started, let's focus on one market.

Where is your market? _____

Whatever market you decide to enter, focus on creating a strategy to be number one in your market. Once you have written down your market here is...

ONE EFFECTIVE MARKETING STRATEGY TO GET YOU STARTED

While I was pursuing my B.S. in Marketing degree, I didn't know when I was going to use the information I'd learned, but my goal was to keep a notebook so I could use my notes as a guide when I needed to apply the information.

TOMEKA PRESCOTT

One marketing strategy in business that has been effective for my small business is postcard mail-outs.

I simply purchase an address list from an online marketing services website, create a postcard about the item or service I'm selling, then mail out the postcard only to people who live in my market.

At the beginning of your business growth, focus on your target market. Later, you can focus on growing in other markets.

You don't have to rush this process because it takes time. I started out with mailing out 100 postcards per month. I did not always do this on a monthly basis. After using this strategy for about one year, I grew a customer database from about 100 customers to about 1000 customers.

In addition to collecting physical mailing addresses and mailing out postcards, ask your customers for their email address so you can sign them up for your email list. Work on building your email list like you would build a physical address database. With one click of the mouse, you can send out newsletters, coupons, and specials to your email database.

Growing a customer database can be fun and rewarding. If you gain a lot of customers via postcard mail-outs and or through sending out coupons via email, and you believe you can't handle them by yourself. I want you to know that you can stop sending out the mail-outs and emails and focus on the customers you currently have.

As a small business owner, you also should know when to slow things down. Business shouldn't be hard or complicated. Your goal is to provide quality services and products to your customers; if you are over swamped with work, it may be hard to focus on your mission and vision. Later in this book I will discuss when it's time to hire employees or outsource a department.

Once you have mapped out your business strategy ...

YOU CAN RESTRUCTURE YOUR BUSINESS STRATEGY

My business strategy changes from time to time. While your business strategy may not be the same as mine, that's okay too. When crafting your business strategy, start small then revamp your business strategy to involve more areas as your business grows.

When the market changes, I revamp my business strategy to change with the market. In business, I have found it challenging keeping up with market trends, so through experience I know if you don't revamp your business strategy as the market changes you can get left behind.

Who wants to get left behind?

BRAINSTORM THEN REVAMP

You should brainstorm before you put effort into revamping your business strategy. You're smart so use the knowledge from within.

TOMEKA PRESCOTT

When you revamp your business strategy, the changes do not always have to be large. It can be as simple as:

- Sending out 25-100 postcards to consumers to test a new market.
- Changing suppliers to get better deals.
- Adding a new service.

I have used a SWOT Analysis to grow my small business. You may already know the definition of a SWOT analysis and you may have already written one or two, but have you implemented a SWOT analysis at your small business?

WHAT IS A SWOT ANALYSIS?

A SWOT Analysis is a tool that can be used by small business owners to help them know where they stand in the market.

It wasn't until my senior year in college that I drafted my first real SWOT analysis. I did it for my family's small business during my marketing internship. I got my notebook and I began to draw out a plan. I wanted to pull out all the internal strengths and weaknesses and external opportunities and threats of the

business. Here is an example of what a brainstorming session may have look like.

FOR INSTANCE FOR THE STRENGTHS I WOULD WRITE:

G Company may have more buying power, but we have fast service.

R Company may have a larger parking lot, but we have created a relaxing environment.

O Company may have more customers, but we have industry knowledge.

W Company may have 50 employees, but we have extra hands through outsourcing.

Next I began to make a list of all the weaknesses, opportunities, and threats such as making a list of every business entering the market. Yes, other businesses entering the market can be a major threat to a small business.

FOR INSTANCE FOR THE WEAKNESSES I WOULD WRITE:

We may have fast service, but we can focus more on branding our name.

We may have created a relaxing environment, but we can focus more on gaining a competitive advantage in new markets.

We may have industry knowledge, but we can focus more on building our customer database.

We may have extra hands through outsourcing, but we can focus more on our business strategy.

FOR INSTANCE FOR THE OPPORTUNITIES I WOULD WRITE:

We can look for ways to expand in new markets.

We can focus on diversity.

We can go global.

We can hire a staff.

FOR INSTANCE FOR THE THREATS I WOULD WRITE:

Similar businesses entering the market.

An over saturated market.

Unable to gain a competitive advantage.

Limited amount of quality suppliers.

Conducting a SWOT analysis may also help with creating a business strategy.

Knowing your internal strengths and weaknesses, and your external opportunities and threats, will help keep you on the right track. A SWOT analysis can be fun to create.

Let's look at a SWOT Analysis I have completed for my small business. While this is not a detailed SWOT Analysis, I want to provide you with an example so you'll know how you can get started to create your very own. You can see that this doesn't have to be complicated.

STRENGTHS:

14 years of industry knowledge.

Offer quality products.

Warm and friendly environment.

WEAKNESSES:

Market the business on only three social media platforms.

No business app.

Limited amount of web-presence.

OPPORTUNITIES:

Add new products to the current product line.

Target a new market.

Create more community projects.

THREATS:

New electronic businesses entering the market.

Corporate retailers with more buying power.

An over saturated market.

YOU CAN USE THIS SPACE BELOW TO MAP OUT YOUR SWOT STRATEGY

Strengths:

-

-
-

Weaknesses:

-
-
-

Opportunities:

-
-
-

Threats:

-
-
-

Now that you've mapped out your SWOT...

IF YOU'VE NEVER WRITTEN A BUSINESS PLAN BEFORE

That's okay!

You can start by creating your business strategy. While this is not a complete business strategy, this template shows how you can

get started. There are a lot of business strategies scattered throughout this book. It's a book all about business success strategies to show what strategies may work best for your business. Continue to implement different strategies as you are growing your business.

BUSINESS PLAN TEMPLATE

If you need help with creating a business plan, don't worry, that's why I am here. I want to help push you forward no matter where you are in business.

TOMEKA PRESCOTT

Do you need a business plan template?

You can visit my website at www.TomekaPrescott.com to download a free business plan template to use as a guide when creating your business plan.

SUMMARY

Create a business strategy that is easy to follow and remember that your business strategy should not be complicated. You can create a well-crafted strategy. Just do it! Don't forget to create a SWOT analysis. The SWOT analysis can be used as a guide throughout the life of your small business.

ONE TIP TO GET STARTED WITH TODAY IF YOU DO NOTHING ELSE.

If you only do one thing after reading this chapter, you should create and map out an outline of your business strategy. You may use the one I have created as a guide to follow. Don't forget to add your own touch of creativity to your business strategy. The end-of-chapter activities can be used as a guide to help grow your business. I encourage you to continue to complete the end-of-chapter activities. Don't forget to keep me updated.

When you have mapped out your business strategy let me know about it: www.TomekaPrescott.com

I am always excited to read business success stories.

Now that you know why the business plan is the heart of your business let's turn to Chapter 3 where we will learn why you don't have to have a million dollar marketing campaign or budget to grow your small business.

FINANCES: DO I NEED INVESTORS? HOW DO I GET FUNDING FOR MY BUSINESS?

WHEN GROWING YOUR SMALL BUSINESS DO YOU THINK YOU NEED MONEY?

I'd say yes, you need money to grow your small business. However, let's look at several ways you can find money.

TOMEKA PRESCOTT

$WHAT YOU'LL LEARN$

This chapter is about finding funds to grow your business and figuring out if you need investors to help grow your business or if you can grow your business debt-free without looking for investors to fund business growth.

As a small business owner, you'll need to be able to fund your growth projects. What project do you plan to create? There is a lot to learn in this chapter so I hope you are ready to create more plans and think strategically.

In this chapter each practical step will help you gain a better understanding of how you can use creative ways to fund business growth projects.

If you have read Chapter 1 you know all about the FOCUS statement. I know what my focus statement says because I have it posted on my wall, right above my desk. Use it now as you learn what you do and don't need at the beginning of your business growth journey.

BREAKING THINGS DOWN

I have a Masters' of Business Administration degree (MBA); I chose to write this book by breaking things down step-by-step so that I would not make things complicated or confuse anyone. I want to see you grow your business and I want you to know a business does not have to be complicated and can be operated debt-free.

TOMEKA PRESCOTT

You don't have to wait until you earn a degree to start growing your business. I started growing a business while I was in college. My goal was to take action and apply the information learned in college and graduate school to real-life business situations.

If you wait to grow your business, remember that you may miss out on opportunities that could have helped push you forward. My focus has not always been on what I could accomplish. My focus is on breaking things down on a daily basis to help me reach larger goals and dreams in life.

YOU DON'T HAVE TO HAVE A MILLION DOLLAR MARKETING CAMPAIGN OR BUDGET

You don't have to have a million dollar marketing campaign or budget to grow your business. When advertising, you can create a basic flyer that tells what you are selling or you can use social media to grow your business without investing a lot of money. Better yet, you can use word-of-mouth to advertise your business. You can be the Million Dollar Campaign—open your mouth, start talking to others about your business and the products and services you offer. I have seen word-of-mouth advertising work year after year. I simply ask my customers to refer a friend, family member, and/or colleague to my business, and they do. They send a lot of people to shop at my store, and I am thankful for the people who refer customers. People like these are the ones who help keep my small business flourishing.

Your goal is to get potential customers to come to your place of business. Once they are there, you can not only tell them about

the products and services you offer, you can show them too. From 20 years of experience in sales, I can tell you that once you notice a potential customer is interested in purchasing your quality products and services, there should not be much you need to do from there. People usually know what they want to purchase and if they have enough money to afford the item they want to purchase. I believe it's okay to help them with their buying purchases.

However, you shouldn't use a pushy sales tactic. Remember that you are not pushing anything. You want to stay focused by listening to your customers and then assisting them during the buying process. If you make your plans carefully, present your "quality" product or service effectively, and sell items that are in demand, you should not have to worry about spending a lot of money promoting the products and services.

Spread the word!

YOU DON'T NEED A LARGE CORPORATE OFFICE

You don't need a large corporate office to be successful in business. You don't need a large facility to get started or even a lot of space to begin growing your business.

TOMEKA PRESCOTT

As long as I have enough space to work, I am good. As long as my customers' have enough space to shop, I am fine with that too. It's not always what you don't have; it's how you use what you do have to grow your small business.

Right now, your goal is to use what you already have to grow your business. I'm not saying you can't have a large corporate office. As you continue to grow your business you'll know when you may need that larger office or need to knock down some walls to make room for your business growth, if you have a physical store or office.

YOU CAN DO IT DEBT-FREE!

When owning and operating a business, being debt-free may help grow your business faster. I would rather operate a debt-free business than have to give the profit to someone else every time I sell a product or service.

TOMEKA PRESCOTT

Personally I would not want to borrow $10,000.00 and then not make a profit and stay in debt. Now you see the importance of self-funding or using creative ways to fund growth projects. It's very important to know how you're going to operate your small business.

Take some time to think about it.

Sometimes we may overthink the process of business growth because we don't have a clear concept of what it means.

When growing your business, don't make it complicated. Remember you should have fun when creating growth for your business, and not have to worry about how you are going to pay someone back.

I operate a debt-free business. You can too.

YOU CAN EARN AND TURN!

I learned this concept from working in my family's business. As my mom would say, "earn and turn." When you earn money from selling products and services, you should turn the money back into the business to continue to grow your business. You should keep earning, and then turning. Do it on a daily basis. This has been a concept that has worked for my small business too. If you stay focused, eventually you should see your business growing, but you have to keep doing it.

This is one reason why it is important to sell products and services that are in demand. If the products and services you sell are in demand, it'll be easier for you to sell the products and services to your customers to earn money to grow your business.

Now that we know what this chapter is about and why it is important, let's learn how to fund small business projects using practical steps.

HOW DO I FUND GROWTH PROJECTS IN PRACTICAL STEPS?

There are several different ways a small business owner can raise capital to fund growth projects.

Can you think of ways to save a certain amount of money to help you fund your growth project?

Is there something you can stop doing? Examples might be running multiple errands throughout the day and going out to

lunch every day. You may want to pack a snack and have lunch at your office. You may find that you're spending too much money to fuel your vehicle when running around too much.

Is there something you can start doing, for example, using technology to streamline processes? To do this you can send an email with your documents attached versus using your long-distance minutes on your office telephone line to fax documents.

You may be able to find extra money from avoiding paying high utility bills at home. When you are not using things simply unplug them. Save the juice to save money.

Think about other ways you can save money and what you can do with the extra money you save.

WHAT I DO

I save extra money in a business savings account from eliminating errands or working an extra hour or two each day. When I decide to fund a growth project, I use the funds from the savings account.

I don't have to put much thought into saving funds for the project other than making sure my business expenses are paid first. I pay most of my major business expenses such as rent, power, internet, and phone bills between the 5th and 7th of every month.

One advantage of using funds from a savings account is that you would not have to pay yourself back if you are unable to gain a profit from the products and services you sell.

If you've already used all of the funds from your savings at start-up, don't worry about this. Just continue to work on earning and

turning your money back into your business and look for other ways to earn money.

YOU CAN DO THIS

SET UP A DISPLAY

Ask a friend or family member if you can set up a display to promote your products and services in their store to advertise your business for a day or a week. You may also want to think about asking your valued customers, too. While I was writing this book, a customer who knew my family came in my store. The customer happens to be a small business owner. I explained that I was about to release my first book. Then the customer informed me that I could set up a display in his store and that he knows a lot of business owners who wouldn't mind doing the same thing as well. I simply asked and now am able to use the money that would have been spent on marketing to fund another business growth project.

Also, I invite small business owners to set up display stations at my place of business to promote their business. I don't ask for any money in return. While this allows a small business owner to gain publicity, it also allows my customers to see products and services other people offer in the town. I am thankful to have great friends to set up displays of their products and/or services at my place of business. Connect with me via social media to let me know your thoughts about setting up displays at businesses and conventions.

www.TomekaPrescott.com

BE A GUEST SPEAKER

Let's keep talking about your business. Ask a small business owner if you could be a guest speaker at an event to promote your products and services. Just introducing yourself and telling the people at the event where you're located and what products and services you sell would be a great start. Continue to be the guest speaker at events, and you may earn extra money while you're promoting your business.

You will probably meet like-minded business owners.

LINK UP WITH A BUSINESS PARTNER IN THE SAME INDUSTRY

Finding ways to advertise your business without spending any money may be challenging. That's why I want to share my business strategies with you. We can overcome challenges together. You may want to link up with a business partner in the same industry. For example, if you are growing a promotional advertising business you can ask your client if you can include your website address or social media page link on the back or side of their business card to say "designed by…." This will help get your name out there without spending money.

PARTNER WITH AN AFFILIATE PROGRAM

Since you are already building your name in the same industry, you can use another company's inventory to help earn additional income for your small business. You can search for affiliates in your industry through an online search engine. Once you find several companies, call them to ask about their affiliate program. See if it will be a great fit for your company, then go from there. Partnering with an affiliate has several benefits.

- No inventory to stock
- Earn commission
- Work at your own pace

Through partnering with affiliate companies, you can even earn residual income to cover business expenses, such as power, cable, rent, and internet. Any percentage amount earned will help grow your small business. I've earned anywhere from 3% to 14% per sale through an affiliate company.

It started with only one customer making repeat purchases.

> *Grow your business slowly; you don't have to grow fast. You're not driving a racecar. You want to drive your small business at a pace you can manage.*
>
> TOMEKA PRESCOTT

LINK UP WITH A FREELANCER IN YOUR INDUSTRY

Link up with a freelancer to contribute articles in your industry to gain publicity. The publicity may bring in more clients to conduct business, which can provide the extra funds to create a growth project.

Remember to always look for alternative ways to save money when growing your business.

Go ahead!

Set up your display, donate your time, be a guest speaker, connect with a fundraiser company, and link up with a freelancer in your industry.

NOT NOW, MAYBE LATER

You may not need investors right now, but you may want to think about it in the future when you plan to build a larger facility for your small business. But know that this, too, can be done through saving.

IF YOU EARNED $1000.00 TODAY HOW WOULD YOU USE IT TO GROW YOUR BUSINESS?

Create a plan that will show how you will use the funds to help grow your business. Remember to create a budget and stick to the budget so you grow your business through strategically planning. I'm always a fan of budgeting and strategically planning to grow my business. You can ask my friends. I am always on a budget and have future plans mapped out. While I don't know my future or know if my plans will stay the same, it is important to create and implement plans to reach goals- especially when you are **wanting to expand your business for growth.**

SUMMARY

Continue to earn and turn and know that you don't have to have a million dollar marketing campaign. Focus on funding growth projects using practical steps. Know that you can be a guest speaker at events to earn extra money to fund growth projects.

As you continue to grow your small business, stay focused on the reason why you're in business. You can do it!

AFTER READING THIS CHAPTER IF YOU LEARN NOTHING ELSE ...

- ➢ Learn the concept of earning and turning.
- ➢ Create a list of ways you can grow your business debt-free.

You can write it down or you can type it out, just as long as you create your list. Remember that you don't give up on growing your small business. You simply keep going and keep growing.

Now let's move on with Chapter 4 to find out why customers are your best assets.

SECTION THREE

Do You Think Customers Are Your Best Assets?

LISTEN TO YOUR CUSTOMERS (LOVE YOUR CUSTOMERS)

Listen to your customers because they are important. You've worked hard to gain them; they didn't fall from a tree.

TOMEKA PRESCOTT

I listen to and love my customers because I know what it feels like to start a business with zero customers.

TOMEKA PRESCOTT

AT START-UP THE ONLY CALLS RECEIVED WERE FROM FAMILY MEMBERS AND FRIENDS

Ring, ring, ring! Hello!

Thank you for calling _____, how may I help you? Is it you, Dad? Yes, it's me. Okay, I thought you were a customer.

Ring, ring, ring! Hello!

Thank you for calling _____, how may I help you? Is this my best friend? Yes, it's me. Do you want to grab lunch later today?

Well, you see! When I began to work for the family electronic business, the only calls received were from family members and friends. Building a customer database took hard work. It took showing up at work every day, not knowing if a customer would call. It took running to the phone because you thought it was a customer, but it was a family member instead. It took making cold calls to try to gain new customers. It was not easy. I am sharing strategies with you in this book to help give you a lift.

As the family business grew, calls started to pick up. So if this is you and your small business, that's okay, I know what it's like not to have customers contacting you when you first start a business. The feeling isn't the best; however, always stay focused.

If the calls or emails are not coming in as you would like, don't get discouraged. It takes time to build a customer database, and even more time to build a database filled with loyal customers. After years being in business, I also know what it's like to have the calls continually roll in. Every time you think you can take a

break, the phone rings, but this is a good thing because you are growing your business.

I know what it takes to expand a customer database, and I'm able to do this well. The strategies I am teaching you throughout this book will help you.

WHAT YOU'LL LEARN ABOUT LISTENING TO AND LOVING YOUR CUSTOMERS

In this chapter, you will learn why customers are important, look at ways customers can help grow your business, learn how to know your customers' needs and wants, find out how to add value to your customers, and learn how to improve customer service.

We will also take some notes so have your pencil/pen and paper ready. Now let's learn why customers are important.

CUSTOMERS ARE IMPORTANT

Customers are your best asset. Without customers you will have no business. My customers have chosen to conduct business at my store; they help me stay in business so I can serve my local community, and they help me grow my business so I can help others.

List three reasons why your customers are important.

- Your customers are important because

  _____.

- Your customers are important because

_____.

- Your customers are important because

_____.

When you have grasped the concept that customers are important, you are well on your way to growing your business. It is not only a good thing to know that customers' are important; it is a good thing to show your customers that they are important. How can you show your customers that they are important? There are several strategies and tips you can use to improve in this area. Continue reading as we dig a bit deeper.

Now you know why your customers are important. Let's look at ways you can show your customers' that they are important by giving them what they really want, which is creating a customer friendly shopping experience. Here are five inside tips for a customer-centered business.

CUSTOMERS ARE YOUR BEST ASSETS SO...

- **Look for ways to save your customers money.**
  Can you offer your customer a discount on a products or service without cutting into your profit? Can you lower your customer's monthly service charge for one or two months as an incentive?

  For example, to give back to my customers I like to discount one electronic accessory item 50% off so my customers can save money.

  When I am out in the market shopping, I am always looking to save money on my purchases. What about you?

I have watched my customers' buying habits day-in and day-out and have come to the conclusion that customers like sales, deals, bargains, and saving money. So your goal here is to find ways to save your customers money throughout the year.

- **Stock up on the items your valued customers purchase.**
  When your valued customers are purchasing the same products and services repeatedly, you should stock up on these items because you know they will not stay in inventory long. So I encourage you to watch your valued customers' buying habits then stock up on the items they are buying.

  Also, it would be good to stock up on items when your vendors and or suppliers have reduced prices. When wholesale prices are reduced, you are able to save money so you can pass on the savings to your customers.

  For example, I stock up on products to sell in my store during the Holiday seasons because this time is when my suppliers offer discounted prices. I then pass on the savings to my customers by lowering prices.

- **Give away a product or service to non-paying or paying customers.**
  Some days I surprise my customers by giving them a free item- just because I value that they are shopping at my retail store.

For example, sometimes I give away free promotional items such as car chargers.

Please make sure you can give away a reasonable item that will not hurt your bottom line. (In Chapter 10 I will discuss how you can strengthen your bottom line). I can do this because I have been in business for several years, and I operate a debt-free business. I've written about the importance of a debt-free business in Chapter 3.

If they buy or don't buy, I still give them a free item. When I give away items, it is random, unless I have a give-a-way at a special event. I don't announce the giving, so the customers who decide to come in my store will not know that they will have a chance at receiving free items. Surprise!

- **Ask your customers how you can improve customer service.**
  Can you improve customer service if you don't know what you need to improve? I believe that your customers can provide strategies and tips to improve in this area.

Just ask them.

Give it a try.

To help out with this, you may want to create a comment box and place it in your store. Your customers can use the comment box to make suggestions to improve customer service.

You may be amazed at how many people will take the time to leave a comment to help you improve customer service.

I have implemented this service in my business, and it does work. It works when I apply the information that I have gained from my customers. Applying the information allows me to see the results. You may not see immediate results but you will never know unless you apply.

- **Have a customer appreciation day.**
  Customer Appreciation days are so much fun and this is why I work hard throughout the year so I can celebrate with my customers. You can have a social, an open house, or a week-long event to celebrate your customers. I like to use all three at my place of business throughout the year.

Next, you'll learn how to practice listening to your customers, getting to know your customers' needs and wants, and adding value to your customers.

HOW TO MAKE YOUR CUSTOMERS LOVE YOU!

Be sweet like cupcakes to your customers.

TOMEKA PRESCOTT

LISTEN TO YOUR CUSTOMERS

Blue one please! I'm sorry we don't have any blue bags. We only sell pink bags. Can I have a green one, I prefer green—it's my

favorite color. I'm sorry the only color we stock is pink. The store down the road may have one, or maybe you can find one online. Type the product you want in the search engine. I prefer to purchase these items from you, I really don't have time to go online and search for items. I would like to purchase these items now; I can't find them anywhere else. Can you please help me? I will even pay for your extra service. Please help me, please!

DON'T IGNORE YOUR CUSTOMERS

As you see, this customer wants to do business with you, and no one else. When you find customers who want to do business with only you, don't ignore them by not listening to what they are telling you.

So, are you really listening to your customers or are you referring them to other places, other stores, or other small businesses?

I am not saying don't share customers with other small business owners, but if you want to grow your business, you have to grab a pen and a piece of paper or a tablet and take notes about what they are telling you so you can help your customers without sending them to other places. I take notes of what my customers are telling me on a daily basis so I can look at ways to help them.

If I can't help them, I'll then refer them to another business.

As small business owners, we may "think" we have a great idea of what our customers may like or want to buy, but in reality it may be challenging to figure out what others like. This is where having good active listen skills can help grow your business. When you are able to master the skills of listening to your customers, you are well on your way to moving to your next level in business.

KNOW THEIR NEEDS AND WANTS

Get to know your customers' needs and wants, then work on finding these items to put in your store or add new services. As a customer, wouldn't it be nice to know that the business owner went the extra mile to find things you like? How awesome is that? I know I would like that very much!

> *I like to really dig in deep when I am learning my customers' needs and wants.*

TOMEKA PRESCOTT

I verbally let my customers know that I am here to serve them and tell them not to be afraid to ask questions about a particular product or service.

If I don't know the answer, I simply tell them that I don't know in a polite way. However, sometimes we are able to solve problems together.

For example, when customers are not sure about how to explain what they want or need, sometimes I am not always able to understand as well. So my goal is to continue to ask questions for clarity, then I look to find similar products and services that may benefit the customer. The customers simply love it when I take the extra effort to help them with their purchases.

DON'T BE AFRAID TO ASK. YOUR CUSTOMERS WILL TELL YOU THEIR NEEDS AND WANTS

I get to know my customers' wants and needs by asking them. I'll say: Can you tell me what type of products you are looking to purchase today, and why? I'll ask them what features they

want to have and why. This allows me to help match my customers with the best products and or services I have to offer at my small business. Remember to get to know your customers' needs and wants.

All customers and clients are not the same. Business owners have to learn how to adapt to the individual customers and/or client's needs and wants. Your goal is to listen to them to find out why they may be interested in your products and services. Then you can be creative in figuring out how to add value. As your business grows, you'll have more customers to listen to.

MASTER THE SKILL OF LISTENING TO YOUR CUSTOMERS

Mastering the art of listening to your customers will make it easier to grow a customer-centered environment, and will help you become a better communicator and small business owner.

While I knew listening to customers is important, it took me several years to master the art of listening to my customers and I am still growing today. No, I am not perfect, but I practice to improve my communication skills daily.

IMPROVE YOUR COMMUNICATION SKILLS DAILY

Whether I am writing a note to a supplier, talking to customer service representatives, and engaging in a conversation with my customers, I am learning as I am communicating. To improve your communication skills, you have to know your weaknesses and work on improving that first.

Once you improve your weak areas of communication, then you can work on sharpening your strengths. Your ultimate goal is to be well-balanced in the area of communication. Having good

communication skills will help build valuable relationships that will then help you continue to grow your business.

Use this space to write about how you plan to improve your communication skills. Go ahead; tell me how you can become a better communicator as a small business owner. Don't be shy.

_____

_____

_____

_____

_____

_____

As you continue to work on improving your communication skills, focus on keeping your loyal customers happy, going the extra mile, greeting customers as they enter your place of business, and helping your customers as much as you can.

KEEP YOUR LOYAL CUSTOMERS HAPPY

People are doing business with you because they like you! Your loyal customers will help keep you in business in many ways. They add value to your business; so always remember to do your utmost to add value to your loyal customers. One time I surprised a customer by letting him pick the prices on any items he wanted in my store. He was shocked and speechless. I told him that I truly valued his business. This customer has been loyal

for several years. When your customers are happy, that's a good thing.

GO THE EXTRA MILE

If you have run five miles in one day, can you go the extra mile by running one more mile? How would you know if you didn't make an attempt to run one more mile?

When helping customers my philosophy is to always go the extra mile to make sure my customers are happy with my products and/or services. When growing a business, sometimes you have to go the extra mile to keep a customer or client. That extra mile could be that hour drive from your place of business to help them, or being an active listener when they don't understand something.

Going above and beyond will help you create loyal customers who will, in turn, also refer their friends, family members, colleagues, and co-workers. If you have gone the extra mile with one customer, the news spreads to other potential customers.

I GO THE EXTRA MILE

I pour my love into my customers, and they love that.

TOMEKA PRESCOTT

While writing this part of the book today, I spent three hours helping one customer with her purchases. I have gone the extra mile for my customers many times. It's a sweet feeling to get a call or a hand-written note from a customer thanking you for

your customer service. This is when I know that my customers value my products and services. I go the extra mile on my bad days and good days. I'm even going the extra mile for you as I am writing this book. I wrote this book for you, and I want you to know that we can work together by sharing business strategies to grow our small businesses together.

I can be found at www.TomekaPrescott.com. It's normal to go the extra mile for others because I have been doing this since I was a kid.

Next, I want you to write down ways of how you plan to go the extra mile and how you plan to add value to your customers.

List four ways of how you will plan to go the extra mile for your customers:

1.
2.
3.
4.

GREET CUSTOMERS AS THEY ENTER YOUR PLACE OF BUSINESS

Greet customers as they enter your place of business and acknowledge when they are leaving. I greet my customers as they enter my store with a hello or hi, and when they leave, I tell them to have a blessed day. I want to let my customers know that I appreciate the fact that they decided to come and shop at my

store. It's not always easy drawing in customers so I appreciate my customers when they do come in to conduct business.

HELP YOUR CUSTOMERS AS MUCH AS YOU CAN

You have to be willing to help your customers as much as you can. When you think you are helping too much, you are off to a good start. Small business owners should have the knowledge and the experience to help the customers who come to conduct business.

Never stop treating your customers with respect, building valuable relationships with your customers, asking your customers for referrals, and thanking your customers for their business.

TREAT YOUR CUSTOMERS WITH RESPECT

➢ Customers should be treated like you would want to be treated.
➢ Don't ignore them when they enter or leave.
➢ Be quick to return phone calls.

It is also important to build valuable relationships with your customers.

BUILD VALUABLE RELATIONSHIPS WITH CUSTOMERS

Relationships are important, so how do you build them? Can you build them in a year or two? Don't fall short it takes longer than that in business. Your customers want to know if you can do what you say you'll do. Don't stop there. Go above and beyond what you can do. Adding value to others may get you into places you have never been before.

ASK YOUR CUSTOMERS FOR REFERRALS

Ask for referrals from your clients and/or customers. Let's say you own a service business where you charge clients a certain amount of money for your services. It is very important to build clientele and ask for referrals. Creating and growing a referral list takes time. This can be done at a slow pace. There is no need to rush things. What if you gain twenty-five new clients solely through referrals from other clients? It would be fantastic, right?

Work on growing your referral list every day; don't ponder yesterday's names and numbers and don't look into the future of how many people you think you can add to your list. Focus on asking for referrals daily and then work your referral list daily by reaching out to the potential clients with the services and/or products you offer. You may collect 25 referrals daily or maybe 100. Right now don't look at the numbers, because even one referral would benefit your business. One customer can become a loyal repeat customer who will continue to help grow your business year after year.

When you create a referral list or a referral program, continue with the program for the life of your business.

You can download a referral list worksheet at:

www.TomekaPrescott.com

Stay tuned because you will start creating your referral list in Chapter 9 when we learn how and why we should create back-up plans to avoid business failure. There is some exciting information ahead, but now keep talking about your business to others to let them know what you are selling. Tell the world who you are and what you do.

TELL YOUR CUSTOMERS THANK YOU!

Letting your customers know that you value their business is a good way to gain repeat business. One way to do this is to give your customer a thank-you card.

You can craft a thank-you note and send it to each customer after a purchase. If you operate a business online, create an electronic thank-you note to post to your social media websites and to send electronically via email. I encourage you to thank your customers for doing business with you. A simple thank you to your customers will go a long way.

SUMMARY

My mom says, "Love and respect your customers. Just be honest. Treat them all the same. This is very important." As you continue to grow your small business, focus on building valuable relationships because you'll never know who can help you get from point A to point B to point C faster than you ever could have imagined.

AN ACTIVITY I WOULD LIKE FOR YOU TO COMPLETE TODAY IF YOU DO NOTHING ELSE

I want you create a worksheet with a list of your loyal customers. Then work on crafting a plan to thank them.

Whether it's a simple thank-you note or a discount on a product and/or service, let your loyal customers know you appreciate their business. Next, let's find out how your business should help

your community be a better place to live. In Chapter 5, we will learn why practicing altruism is important.

Chapter 5

PRACTICE ALTRUISM
UNSELFISH REGARD TOWARDS
OTHERS

Help people who are in need. Let them lean on you. Hold them up. Hold their hands. Walk with them. Don't let them fall. Be their light.

TOMEKA PRESCOTT

MY MOM FOUNDED AN ELECTRONIC CELLULAR PHONE WIRELESS STORE

My mom, Mary C. Prescott, founded her electronic cellular phone wireless store (Prescott Wireless) by helping others. One hot summer day we were at a client's house. We had just come back from helping an elderly client grocery shop.

She asked the customer if there was anything else she could help with. The customer said yes, I would like to have one of those things you are using to talk on—which was a cellular phone. My mom delivered a cellular phone to this customer the next day, and when she did that, others in the household asked for one as well.

My mom then took advantage of this opportunity by launching an electronic cellular phone store. She was able to jump in the industry in the early 2000's.

In the early 2000's it was tough to land a contract with a cellular phone company. She was turned down a few times before she received a contract.

One thing she didn't do was give up.

My mom has always been an entrepreneur, selling things from cosmetics to home improvement items such as decks and fences.

MY MOM BUILT A BUSINESS FROM SCRATCH

With her entrepreneurship background, she was able to build a cellular phone business from scratch.

It only took the will to help one client and one gifted and motivated businesswoman to create a business that is still growing.

WE HELPED

My dad and siblings all helped grow the small business. I can say that we are all tech savvy. Countless hours were spent working to market the business, sharing knowledge, building valuable relationships with suppliers and vendors, providing customer service, building relationships to gain loyal customers (we have some customers that have been with us since day 1), and serving our local community.

As I write this book, we are still connecting, sharing, and serving to grow the small business on a daily basis. What are your thoughts about connecting, sharing, and serving while growing your small business?

MY MOM SIMPLIFIED COMPLEX INFORMATION

Air time? What is air time? In the early 2000's there were a lot of people who didn't understand the meaning of this term. Air time is a term that means cellular phone minutes (talk time). My mom simply called it minutes. She was able to break down complex information that may have been confusing to others. She really wanted the information to be understood by all. This helped her continue to grow her business.

While in college, I would create flyers using terms that I learned while pursuing a Marketing degree. My mom would ask me to reword the information so customers were not confused. This was when I learned the importance of keeping the information on flyers simple and short. For example: Do you need a cellular phone? If yes, you can contact us at: www.PrescottWireless.com

I model this same concept at my business when advertising my products and services and while talking to my customers and to

the students I teach. The question I always ask myself is how can I break a concept or information down into its simplest form?

MY MOM LOVED HELPING OTHERS

To help others you have to have open ears to listen to people, and then a kind heart to help them all that you can.

TOMEKA PRESCOTT

This is what this term means and this is what this means is what I would hear my mom teaching me as I followed her on business appointments when I was a child. While going door-to-door talking to clients, I noticed my mom was doing more than selling a product or service. She was practicing altruism. What does altruism mean? Altruism can be defined as not being selfish towards other people.

At the time, I did not know the meaning of this term, but now I do. We would spend hours, days, weeks, months, and years helping people who were in need of assistance, still do today, and will continue to help others. You may have heard once before that learning is a life-long process. I agree with that statement. I also want to say that helping others is a life-long process.

As a reminder, when you help others, they help you too!

So don't be afraid to give a helping hand.

MY MOM GIVES BACK TO THE LOCAL COMMUNITY

Fall in love with community service.
Right where you live.

TOMEKA PRESCOTT

My mom gives back to the local community. As a business owner, you have several responsibilities and one is building up your local community by giving back. As you continue to build and grow your business, step-by-step, create a plan for social responsibility as well. This plan could include customer appreciation events, fund raising events, and much more. Whether it's an in-house event created by you or a community event you plan to participate in—have fun!

SOCIAL RESPONSIBILITY IS A SMALL BUSINESS OWNER RESPONSIBILITY

When your battery dies in your car, you give it a
boost to jump-start your car. I want you to be
the boost that jump-starts your local community
because social responsibility is important.

TOMEKA PRESCOTT

➢ You have the power to lift up your local communities.
➢ You can create a business that revolves around social responsibility.
➢ You can make the difference in your local community.
➢ You can change the world to make it a better place to live.

Now let's see how you can do this in practical steps.

HOW CAN YOU HELP THE PEOPLE IN YOUR LOCAL COMMUNITY?

Community projects are the backbone of my business. Seeing the community projects grow is my vision.

TOMEKA PRESCOTT

You can use your talent, skills, and knowledge to give back to the community. Giving back does not necessarily mean that you need to donate money. Some other ways to give back are to donate time, things you no longer need that are sitting around your house, or business knowledge and skills. So let's join together as a team to practice altruism. How can you give back?

In practical steps, this is what you can do.

Start a community project at your place of business. You may want to collect coats to give away during the cold months or donate money or food to a local food shelter.

I spend a lot of time teaching students in my ethics classes about the importance of giving back to help make their communities a better place to live. As a teacher, I lead by example so I also spend a lot of time implementing the things I teach my students about ethics and how important it is for people to get involved in their local communities. I want to share with you my current community projects as well as projects I plan to implement in the future. To follow any of my projects, you can visit my website at: www.TomekaPrescott.com

CURRENT PROJECTS:

- The Education Project
- The Recycling Project
- The Thank You Project
- The Food Project

FUTURE PROJECTS:

- The Reading Project
- The Writing Project
- The Hospital Project
- The Business Project

I am always open to any ideas or suggestions. All I want to do is help make my community a better place to live, so that is why I focus on giving back to the local community. I stay focused, and I don't stop. Hopefully one day I will be able to reach people all around the USA and other countries with these same projects.

EDUCATION PROJECT

This project started with my family business giving away pencils, loose-leaf paper, and spiral notebooks to people who needed the extra help. I then went on to give away seasonal pencils during the different holidays every year. I didn't give much. I started giving away 12 pencils seasonally, then each year I would give more. When you have a heart to give anything you are doing the right thing.

This small project started when I was a kid. As I got older I never stopped giving away these items. Twenty-plus years later, this project still grows each and every year.

You don't have to start big - you can start small. This project continues to help school children in my local community. I have plans to continue to grow this project and expand to help school children in my state, other states, and countries. While I am not there yet, I am moving. Recall what you learned in Chapter 1. I am keeping my eyes on the ball. I am staying focused.

Have you thought of a project you could start? Maybe this project relates to the products and services you provide. If you are in the sporting industry, you might create a project where you donate basketballs or footballs to your local recreational department.

This is just an idea. Get creative with this because you never know who you could make smile or you never know who you can inspire or simply help.

You can use this section to brainstorm.

Project idea one:

Project idea two:

Project idea three:

Project idea four:

Project idea five:

Now that you've created your project ideas, be the one who grows your local community, take the lead.

Now let's look at my recycling program - nothing difficult you see - no extravagant name.

RECYCLING PROGRAM

I recycle and I have fun recycling to help make the world a better place to live.

I helped created a recycling program in my local community. Recycling to help make the world a better place to live has always been dear to my heart. My friends know how excited I get when it comes to recycling.

If an item is recyclable, I will recycle it.

Value can be added to your business by getting involved in recycling. In the recycling program, I allow customers to recycle their unused cellular phones, batteries, and electronic accessories, such as car chargers and wall chargers, and allow them to receive a free car charger per item they recycle.

The limit is one per year and my customers love this added value incentive. It helps keep the environment clean, as well as allows customers to save money by not having to purchase a car charger to charge their cellular phone on the go.

The recycling program is a year round project. You can create a recycling program and add it to your small business too!

Now, how do you plan to create your recycling program? You can get started now.

What items are recyclable in your business?

1.

2.

3.

Here's a list of recyclable items at my business:

Cellular phones

Cellular phone accessories

Ink cartridges

Where can you recycle the items?

1.

2.

3.

Where do I recycle items?

I recycle items at a local recycling center. You can follow my recycling project at: www.TomekaPrescott.com

What type of in-house recycling program you can create for your business?

1.

2.

3.

What are your action steps? Let's get moving!

1.

2.

3.

What programs have I created for my small business?

A drop-off center and I use recyclable business cards, and have created recycling incentives for my customers.

THE THANK-YOU PROJECT

This project is implemented every November at my small business. I use several ways to thank my customers during this month. I give out thank-you cards, verbal thank-you's every day, and I also give away electronic gadgets to simply thank my customers for their business.

How can you thank your customer? List some strategies here:

1.
2.
3.
4.
5.

THE FOOD PROJECT

This is a yearlong project where food items such as canned goods and money are donated to the people who are in need.

My future plans for my other projects are:

THE READING PROJECT

I have plans to write and publish a series of children books to help children improve their reading skills. Currently I also donate my time by reading books to preschoolers throughout the year.

THE WRITING PROJECT

Writing is important and has also been something that is dear to my heart. In this project, I want to mentor children and adults to help them improve their writing skills.

THE HOSPITAL PROJECT

In this project, I want to share my love by donating blankets and stuffed animals to people who are in the hospital.

THE BUSINESS PROJECT

In this project, I plan to focus on helping others grow their business.

> *In addition to giving back to your community,*
> *always be kind to your customers and be happy!*
>
> TOMEKA PRESCOTT

BE KIND TO YOUR CUSTOMERS

While it is very important for you to generate income by selling your products and services, a business is more than that.

Being nice to others will take you a long way in business. I want you to have an unselfish regard.

It's the right thing to do. Let them know you value their business. In Chapter 7, I will share some strategies about how you can add value to your customers. Always see what you can give, because when you have a giving heart, you'll be blessed. Focus on being

happy too, because it's simply another way to grow your business. Love what you do! You will be able to pass on the love to others.

BE HAPPY!

When you are happy, you can make others happy, too! So, love what you do and know who you are.

Being happy means so much to me. I enjoy the simple things of life - like the beautiful flowers in the spring, the beautiful sunshine in the summer, the snow in the winter, and the leaves in the fall. I am a person of all seasons.

Enjoying the weather in all seasons is what makes me happy, and I know it. I also enjoy making homemade ice cream, and eating it too. I want to encourage you to know what makes you happy. Love it and hug it; you should love to do the things that make you happy.

Knowing what makes you happy can actually help you be more excited about operating your small business. When you're happy, you are able to create an environment of happiness that will hopefully spread to your employees, vendors, suppliers, customers, and the list goes on. It can help you have that unselfish regards towards other people.

How can you create an environment of happiness at your small business?

- _____
- _____
- _____

- _____
- _____
- _____
- _____
- _____
- _____
- _____
- _____
- _____
- _____

INSIDE TIP: I do this by coming to work energized and knowing what I want to accomplish for that day.

My happiness spreads to others. Throughout the day, I help my customers to the best of my ability and let them know that I am here to help serve them. I've been asked "Why are you so happy?" It's because I enjoy living.

SUMMARY

Create a business environment that is built upon having an unselfish regards towards other people. Help build up your community to make it a better place to live by creating community projects through your small business. Be generous and give back.

Practice being kind to all of your clients and customers, and simply be a happy small business owner. Be a mentor, and hold out your hands to help people in need.

BE HAPPY IF YOU DON'T DO ANYTHING ELSE AFTER READING THIS CHAPTER AND...

I want you to write one paragraph to explain what makes you happy. Then write one paragraph to explain how you can make your customers happy.

Join me in Chapter 6 where you'll learn how to find your niche!

SECTION FOUR

Stand Out From the Competition

Notes:

FIND YOUR NICHE AND OFFER QUALITY PRODUCTS AND SERVICES

WHY IS BEING VISIBLE IN YOUR MARKET IMPORTANT?

Come on and hang out with me while I share my story about my trip to São Paulo, Brazil and what I have learned from visiting another country.

TOMEKA PRESCOTT

VISITING THE CITY OF SÃO PAULO, BRAZIL

Visiting the city of São Paulo, Brazil, one summer was a unique learning experience. I was there with my college soccer team on a mission trip for a couple of weeks. In the city

of São Paulo, it seemed like everybody was an entrepreneur or some type of business owner.

People were out in the streets selling hotdogs, bracelets, t-shirts—you name it. The one thing I noticed was a lot of entrepreneurs were selling the same items, just steps away from each other. They were so close to each other that it reminded me of how vendors are set up at a flea market, or jockey lot.

I learned a lot that day in Brazil.

I learned…

- In a market that is overcrowded, you have to learn how to adapt to the market while creating ways to stand out.
- Creating profitability in such a tight market may be challenging; however, you can create a competitive advantage by offering different services.
- You should not worry about the competition; you should focus on improving your small business.

Also, I realized that day in Brazil…

TO SUCCEED YOU HAVE TO BE DIFFERENT

You have to change your mindset and know that you have the knowledge and power to make things happen. You have to put yourself around other business-minded people to help get yourself to the next level. You have to push all negativity aside and create a strategy before you go to the market.

Once you take your strategy to the market, you have to work your strategy, and when you have finished working your strategy, you have to do it again. In Chapter 2, I shared one effective marketing strategy to help you get started.

Back to the market in Brazil.

I was not in the market for shopping that day. I was out sightseeing; however, if I were shopping I would have purchased items from vendors with the added value deals. For example, I can recall one guy selling two bracelets for the price of one to stand out. So instead of selling one bracelet for 11.93 Brazilian Real (5.00 U.S. dollars), he added value by selling two bracelets for the price of one.

Did he get all the business? Well I'm not really sure, but it looked like he did. He went a bit further than others; he did not just sit around on his blanket or mat and think that business was going to magically grow before his eyes. He got up, went to the consumers in the market, and asked if they wanted to buy his products.

While there were so many people out there selling the same stuff, in business you have to go after your sale; if you want to win in business, go get it! Go with what you have because you can always get better and add new things to your service or product line-up later. But remember, don't use the push sales tactic.

HOW YOU CAN STAND OUT IN ANY MARKET

This chapter is about finding your "niche" products and services and selling quality products and services to stand out. Simply, a niche product or service can be defined as a product or service that is different from the other products and services in the same market and is needed or wanted by the consumer.

The consumers of your products and services are people who buy your products and services to use. Once you find your niche

product and/or service and find consumers to purchase these, you are on your way to growing your business.

In this chapter, you will learn why quality is important. Whether you are selling a service or a product, quality matters. You will also go on a journey with me as I show you how I find the best quality products and services and how I look for ways to be different in my market.

While I have a strategy in place of standing out in my market, I want to teach you how you can stand out in any market. You want to be seen, right? There are strategies to help you become more visible in an economy where the market might be saturated, meaning that many people are selling what you are selling.

COMPETITION IS ALL AROUND YOU

Competition is beside you; it's at your backdoor. It's at the corner store. Oh, and there is even more. It's in the online market for sure.

TOMEKA PRESCOTT

With competition all around, you must create a way to be different from your competitors. If you believe your competition may be far away or does not exist, you must still create a way to be different because you never know when the new online business may launch or when the new business may open across the street from you, offering the same products and services you sell.

This happens all the time in business, and when you, the small business owner, do not have a plan created to gain a competitive

advantage, you may have to work harder to compete in your industry to grow your business in any economy.

Here is what I think about the competition. To create a competitive advantage you should focus on being your personal best in business. I really don't think about the competitors in the market because I believe that we should all work together as a team to help build communities. Deep down inside I do the best that I can do to grow my small business. I focus on improving my customer service and product and service options so I can continue to grow my vision. If all business owners have the "vision" to build up their local communities, this would be amazing.

❖

HAVE FUN WITH THE CREATIVE SIDE OF BUSINESS

I have several years of hands-on experience working in the business industry. I have learned that you have to be willing to try new things and have fun with the creative side of business.

I am always looking for creative ways to do something. For example, I like to create in-house advertising flyers and promotional materials to market my small business. What makes me successful in business is being creative.

You have to be different. Period.

Especially if you want to hang out with the big businesses. Business is more than selling a product or service to a consumer. No matter where you live in the world, you can be creative in business to stand out.

***Now spice up your business, be creative,
and stand out in your market!***

TOMEKA PRESCOTT

Now you know that competition is all around you and that you should be creative in business to gain a competitive advantage. Think about your plans to gain that competitive edge in your market.

GAINING A COMPETITIVE ADVANTAGE IN YOUR MARKET

How do you plan to gain a competitive advantage in your market? How can you find ways to generate more business income? How can you grow a successful business? When I think of the word "create" I think of making something original. When you think of the words "stand out" what is the first thought that comes to your mind? Now hold that thought while we explore ways to help make your business better. We will look at quality first.

FIRST, FIND YOUR NICHE PRODUCTS AND SERVICES

Offering niche products and services will allow you to stand out by selling things that no one else is selling so that consumers will have to come to you.

When you find that "niche" product and/or service, the big retailers and businesses will refer customers to you. I have experienced this over and over again. Receiving a call from the

big retailers to see if I carry a product or service to help their customer is amazing because I am a small business owner.

You'll think that the big retailers would have or could get the items their customers need and want. However, this is not always the case. When you find your niche products and services, the word will spread. Once it does, it's always good to have another back-up plan because usually you'll notice others offering your niche products and/or services soon or later. I have seen this happen repeatedly.

I guess that's what secret shoppers are for. This is what I have experienced in business and I want you to know that this can happen. So continue to have plan A, B, C, and D. Think strategically.

SELF-EDUCATION WILL HELP YOU

Who knows your learning style better than the one who is learning?

TOMEKA PRESCOTT

When you are looking for your niche product and/or services, self-education is important. You don't have to know everything, but make sure you are well educated in your industry. This will help you understand whether the products you find or the services you create will be a possible niche or not.

Technology can help you get self-educated.

From online videos to online learning workshops, you can access information that can help grow your business by conducting research online. Get to searching! It's fun! You don't have to

search alone. If you have any employees, involve them in the researching process.

When you are conducting research, look at trends in your local area, in other states, and countries. Sometimes you may gain more knowledge by researching globally. If you own a sporting shop, don't be afraid to know what small business owners internationally are selling in their sporting stores. You never know, you may find your niche product or service in another country.

When you learn how to self-educate, you are able to gain knowledge about topics you may have not learned in school or in other learning environments.

YOU CAN SUBSCRIBE TO MAGAZINES, NEWSLETTERS, READ BOOKS, AND BLOGS

If you want to find your niche products and services, you have to keep up with your industry. I do this by subscribing to magazines, newsletters, and by reading books and blogs. With the use of technology, industries change fast. What you are able to sell one month might not sell the next month. You never know and that's why you should plan ahead to learn all you can.

To keep up with me, you can join my mailing list at:

www.TomekaPrescott.com

On my website, I will provide tips of how you can continue to gain knowledge in any industry.

NEXT LOOK TO SEE WHAT PRODUCTS AND SERVICES YOUR COMPETITORS ARE SELLING

You can start by creating a list of the products and services your competitors are selling. Then you can see how to add value to those products and/or services.

COMPETITOR'S PRODUCTS

Product 1

Product 2

Product 3

Product 4

Product 5

COMPETITOR'S SERVICES

Service 1

Service 2

Service 3

Service 4

Service 5

Next, think of what you can do to add value to the products and services your competitors are selling.

We have touched on the importance of listening to your customers in Chapter 4. Continue to practice listening to your customers.

LISTEN TO YOUR CUSTOMERS

What you may think is good, another person may have a better idea. If you can't think of that niche product or service you need to offer—maybe a customer can. What are your thoughts about this?

Don't forget to…

ASK SUPPLIERS AND VENDORS, TOO

Sometimes I am able to find niche products and services by asking the suppliers and/or vendors for their latest and best selling items. However, I always keep in mind that I must have a general idea to know if my customer will buy the product and services in my market. Because it is a good seller for the supplier, does not mean it will be a good seller for my business. There were products that I thought could be niche items, but weren't. Now that you know how important it is to find niche products and services, let's look at ways to find quality products and services.

❖

HOW OFTEN SHOULD YOU BE LOOKING FOR NICHE PRODUCTS AND SERVICES?

I know you may be wondering how often you should be looking for these niche products and services. You should create a plan to look for these products and services daily, because you will never know when your "niche" product or service is not really a "niche" product or service in your area, market, or industry anymore. When the market becomes saturated, you will have a plan in place that will keep you moving forward. This is why I

talk about making strategic plans in this book. Always have a back-up plan. A plan A, B, C, and D, and so forth.

BENEFITS OF OFFERING NICHE PRODUCTS AND SERVICES

Offering a "niche" product or service will drive customers to your business. Maybe not overnight, but if you work on finding your "niche," your business will grow. So always remember to find your niche products and services and offer them to your customers because it is important. You'll have a special group of customers coming to you to buy these items because they can't find them anywhere else locally.

How would you feel to know your small business is the only business in the area with a special niche product or service? I'd feel great because I'll know I put in hard work to find these products or have created special services for my customers to add value. I'm always all in for adding value to my customers and my business. If I can do this by offering niche products and/or services, I will continue to work hard to find niche products and/or services. As you continue to read, we'll learn more about adding value to others in the next chapter.

SECOND, SELL QUALITY PRODUCTS AND SERVICES

To find quality products to offer, I find asking the supplier's sales representative about the quality of products they offer to be a good start. The vendors I have worked with have stocked the same products, but different quality. I like to really dig in and compare the differences by asking a lot of questions. Sometimes I know my suppliers and vendors wonder why I'm asking all of

these questions. My answer is because I want to provide the top of the line products and services to my customers.

First I ask the suppliers and vendors general questions about the quality of their products.

- What is the lifespan of the product?
- Are there a lot of returns for this product?
- What products are your other customers buying?
- Have you used this product? If yes, what are your thoughts about the quality?
- I notice this same product is made by different companies. Which company produces the best product?
- Does this product come with a manufactory warranty?
- Does this product come with a supplier warranty?
- Is this product durable?
- Is this a quality product?
- Can you explain the benefits of the product?
- Is this item a hot seller?
- What is the quality difference between your low quality and high-quality product?
- Can you provide me with the product specifications?
- If I don't like the quality of the item, what is the return policy?

Second I purchase the items and test them out for myself. To test items I use them on a daily basis. If I don't have any problems with the product and if I think it is durable, I will order more of the products to stock in my store. If the item is good, I order more of the item; if the item is of poor quality I don't order the item.

Third I do not bounce from vendor to vendor and supplier to supplier. Once I find quality vendors and suppliers, I continue to purchase inventory from them. There are a couple of vendors that I have been conducting business with for over 13 years.

All in all, my goal is to find the best quality products and services for my customers. Once this goal is reached, I am happy. While it is important to find quality products and services, it is also important to use quality packaging to sell those products and services. Next, we will talk about the quality of packaging.

THIRD, QUALITY PACKAGING

Your packaging should use its non-verbal communication skills to talk to your customers.

TOMEKA PRESCOTT

When looking for quality products, you also want to look for quality packaging. You should create a plan to be the best business with the best packaging. Whether you are packaging products and/or services, the packaging should speak for itself without you saying a word- even though I know packaging cannot verbally say "I look good and I know it!"

However, non-verbal communication is important. This is why you should dress your products for success. Most of the suppliers I purchase my inventory from offer in-house packaging where I can have my business logo added to all packaging for an additional cost. I don't always go this route. Finding someone who has keen knowledge with packaging is a good strategy.

If you would like help with designing packaging, you can outsource this task. Sometimes a designer may have a better eye

than you! This will allow you to stay focused on your business. I will go into more details about outsourcing departments in Chapter 12.

As I am writing this book, I am planning what type of packaging for my book to send to my customers who order directly from me. Sometimes I find myself so focused on packing, you'd think I am selling packaging with no product inside.

This is not the case; however, I understand how important it is to always use quality packaging when packaging your products to sell to consumers.

It is also a good idea to package the services you offer too. How can you package your services? Creating a brochure and flyer that list the services you offer is a good way to package services. If you are selling your services online, you can create flyers and newsletters.

❖

INSIDE TIP: Don't ever give up on finding the best quality products and services to offer to your customers. Once you realize how important quality is, you are well on your way to growing your business.

The key here is that offering quality products and services and finding your niche product and services will help you stand out in your market. I hope you found these strategies useful! Also, don't ever give up on creating the best quality packaging.

Let your packaging help sell your quality products and/or services. You can do it!

ONCE YOU FIND YOUR NICHE PRODUCTS AND SERVICES KEEP TALKING ABOUT YOUR BUSINESS

Don't ever give up on talking about the products and/or services you sell. Let's say you write and sell an eBook online to tell the world about your sporting business. You are all excited about launching your first eBook; you promote your new eBook before the launch to friends, colleagues, and family members to get them interested in purchasing your book. After you launch your eBook, the sales roll in. By the end of the third month you have sold over 500 copies of your eBook; then sales stop rolling in so you stop thinking about creating buzz about your newly release eBook. You finally give up marketing your eBook due to low sales.

When you create a product or service that does not sell as you've expected, don't give up on telling people who you are and what you do. This one product or service does not define the other products and/or services you may sell in the future.

Giving up because one product or service doesn't sell well is not the best thing to do when you are in business. Whether you are making sales or not, you should continue to market your new eBook because you never know when someone is in the market looking for what you are selling. There are strategies you can use without spending money.

What do you do if the eBook is still not selling after promoting through advertising and branding? While we want all of our products and services to sell, sometimes you will have those items that won't sell. That's okay. You can always add new

products to your inventory or create new services. Think innovate! What are your thoughts about this?

SUMMARY

I want your small business to be visible in your local market. I want people to know who you are and what you sell. Remember to always look for niche products and services so you can continue to stand out in your market. Be creative. You can do it!

AFTER READING THIS CHAPTER IF YOU DON'T READ ANYMORE I WANT YOU TO...

Find that "niche" product or service you can sell to add to your business. If you already believe you may have that "niche" product or service, that's great! However, I want you to find another "niche" product or service. This is going to take a lot of thinking and researching—don't give up!

You can download a niche product and service worksheet at www.TomekaPrescott.com to help you get started.

Were you able to find your niche products and services?

I hope so!

Let's keep moving to Chapter 7 where we will learn how to add value to your business to gain a competitive advantage.

Chapter 7

ADD VALUE TO YOUR BUSINESS TO GAIN A COMPETITIVE ADVANTAGE. I VALUE YOU!

I value that you have chosen to become a small business owner. I value that you help others by matching them with products and/or services to fulfill their needs and wants.

I value that you are living your dreams (if you've always dreamed of becoming a small business owner).

There is a reason why you are a small business owner.

There is a reason you provide the products and/or services you sell to consumers.

There is a reason you may spend countless hours marketing your products and services to potential customers.

There really is a reason; however, I want you to know the reason you are in business. Once you know the reason you are a small business owner, focus on ways you can add value to your small business. You may already have learned what drives me as a small business owner. I want you to carry out your mission and vision to inspire others to do the same as a small business owner.

THIS IS THE VALUE CHAPTER

This chapter is about learning how to add value to your business to gain a competitive advantage in your market. It's about learning what adding value is all about. You will explore strategies I implement to add value to my small business to continue to grow my business. Also you will learn how to be creative with the process of adding value to your small business and you will learn how adding value to your small business can help you stand out as a small business owner.

Throughout this chapter, you will gain an invaluable amount of information about adding value to your small business and you will learn how to do this in simple practical steps. In this chapter, I want you to answer the questions, so grab your pen and paper. This allows you to put your thoughts on paper.

At the end of the chapter, you will have the opportunity to write a paragraph or two to explain how you're going to add value to your business.

We've learned why your customers are your most important assets in Chapter 4 so if you haven't read it yet, go back a few chapters. It's loaded with valuable information.

THE POWER OF ADDING VALUE

First, add value to the people who come in contact with you; they may add value to you. Then you both can add value to someone else. Next, they can add value to someone new. Last, you'll realize that you've created an environment that fosters adding value.

TOMEKA PRESCOTT

Adding value to your business helps the business become more noticeable in a market that is overcrowded and/or saturated.

Can you picture being a small business owner who is well-known in your market?

Do you want to be recognized in your industry for adding value to others?

As a business owner, it's important to know why adding value to your small business is important. By adding value to your small business, you will be able to continue to grow your business. You will be able to continue to inspire other business owners to grow their business. Also, you will be able to continue to gain a competitive advantage in your market.

As a small business owner, I like to add value to my customers, potential customers, employees, products, services, suppliers and vendors, mail carriers, people who I meet in the market, people in general, and, oh yes, the business environment.

Now let's see how you can add value to your business in a few practical steps.

MY HEART OF ADDING VALUE: ADD VALUE TO YOUR CUSTOMERS.

☞ LISTENING TO AND LEARNING FROM YOUR CUSTOMERS

First, listening to and learning from your customers will add value to your business. It is important to learn how to listen to your customers. While they are in your store or either in your presence, listen to what they are saying before, during, and after completing a sale. I practice listening to my customers on a daily basis and implement some of the advice they offer. This has helped me learn how to add value to my customers. For example, I know how much my customers love the events and socials that are held at my place of business throughout the year so I ensure I create a lot of events for them to come and have a good time.

☞ CELEBRATE YOUR BUSINESS SUCCESS WITH YOUR CUSTOMERS

Second, you can add value to your customers by celebrating your business success with customers through hosting new product and service launch parties. Also, you can invite your customer to a business social to simply have fun without marketing your products and/or services.

☞ CELEBRATE DURING THE HOLIDAY SEASONS WITH YOUR CUSTOMERS

Third, the Christmas holiday season is an exciting time of the year. During the Christmas holiday seasons I like to give gifts to my customers and to the people who have helped me

throughout the year. This is a second way I like to add value to my customers. Wouldn't you like a gift? I would.

The annual Christmas Party is an event I have at my business every year. Each year this event continues to grow and change. Be merry and give!

☞ OFFER YOUR CUSTOMERS A FREE GIFT WITH PURCHASE

Fourth, you can offer your customers a free gift with the purchase of any item or service. It's that simple. For example, if a client purchases a service from you, you can offer them a free promotional gift-card with purchase.

It does not matter if you operate a retail business or a service-based business, or even an online business, there are plenty of ways you can be creative to add value to your business throughout the year. Next we will learn how you can add value to potential customers because they might become your customer one day. So why not treat them like a valued customer?

ADD VALUE TO POTENTIAL CUSTOMERS

When adding value to my small business I like to add value to consumers who are not my customers yet because you never know when potential consumers may become your customers.

TOMEKA PRESCOTT

☞ PROVIDE POTENTIAL CUSTOMERS WITH RESOURCES

I encourage you to provide potential customers with resources to let them know who you are and what products and services you sell. You can give your potential customers your business card, either a print business card or an electronic card, so they'll have your contact information if they need or want your products and/or services. You can also provide potential customers with knowledge about a product and/or service they may be interested in purchasing or you can leave them with a brochure of your products and/or services with prices included to help provide them more information that may help them make a decision.

☞ INVITE YOUR POTENTIAL CUSTOMERS TO SOCIALS AND EVENTS

Invite your potential customers to socials and events so they don't miss out on all of the fun stuff! I know as a consumer I like to drop in to shop with small business owners who invite me to socials and events held at their place of business. I have even dropped in at events held online too. I love online events because I don't have to leave my house. I can stay at home and explore what's new in the market.

INSIDE TIP: Don't forget to create events that can be held online for potential customers. These can be events such as what's new in the market, where you inform consumers about the latest gadgets or services being offered.

Provide your customers with free promotional items of your products and/or services to see if they might be interested in

buying from you. This is a great way to start to build a relationship with potential customers. When you allow your potential customers to sample your products and/or services without spending any cash, you are able to add value to your potential customers. So think about what you can give away to potential customers. I like to offer my potential customers free products and services.

Make your list here: What can you offer to your customers free of charge?

-
-
-
-

How often can you offer this product or service? On a daily basis or a monthly basis? Think about this—it's a great way to add value!

☞ GIVE AWAY GIFT CARDS

You can give away gift cards to your potential customers.

You don't have to start with a large amount.

In my business I give away branded $5.00 gift cards to potential customers. The gift cards are very cute. My business logo sits on front of the card.

I also give these gift cards to my customers too. Adding value to potential customers will help you continue to build a business that values others and will help you to continue to gain a competitive advantage in your market.

You're in business to help others, right? So why not help the people who are not your customers, too? Now that we have learned why it's important to add value to the people who are not your customers, take a look at how you can add value to your WONDERFUL employees! Employees should have value added too.

☞ ADD VALUE TO EMPLOYEES

Employees are amazing, so value their knowledge and skills.

TOMEKA PRESCOTT

Adding value to your employees will also add value to your small business. As I know from experience of being an employee at several companies, I really enjoyed when employers awarded employees with incentives such as gas cards and paid time off.

It makes you feel special, right?

☞ PROCESS ERROR-FREE PAYROLL CHECKS ON TIME

I add value to my employees, which adds value to my small business.

You can do this by paying your employees on time. I like to process payroll one day or two before the payroll due date to ensure my employees will get paid on time.

I also double-check for any errors. While I'm not an HR specialist, I understand the importance of getting the payroll right the first time.

☞ SURPRISE YOUR EMPLOYEES WITH GIFT CARDS

You can add value to your employees by surprising them with gift cards to their favorite restaurants and/or favorite place to eat. On a side note, you can reward yourself with these gift cards too. If you don't motivate yourself, who will? It's something to think about.

☞ IMPLEMENT YOUR EMPLOYEES' FEEDBACK

You can add value to your employees by listening to your employees' feedback throughout the day.

If a process can be streamlined and made easier, why not go for it. That's why I always ask my employees to tell me what I can do to better my small business.

When feedback is received, I acknowledge the message then think to see if the business can benefit from the feedback. If yes, I implement what I have learned. If no, then I collaborate with my employees to see what a good fit for the business is, then go from there.

I am not a hard person to get along with so most of the time the feedback will get implemented. If it works, we continue to work at getting better. If it doesn't work, we think of other ways to improve.

☞ GIVE INCENTIVES TO YOUR EMPLOYEES

Some people may be motivated to perform job tasks by an internal motivation without non-physical incentives. This is a type of motivation that comes from within. For example, expressing my words to you on paper, and being able to share

my knowledge with you, motivated me to continue to write and publish this book.

Some people may be motivated to perform job tasks by external motivation by receiving a physical incentive such as a bonus, a gas gift card, or a food gift card. Don't you enjoy being motivated by incentives?

These are some incentives I give to my employees:

> ➢ Words of encouragement.
> ➢ A high-five.
> ➢ A food gift card.
> ➢ A bonus.

Are you motivated by any of the above incentives? Take some time to write what motivates you. You then can use this as a guide to survey your employees to figure out how they are motivated to perform job tasks and duties. Knowing how your employees are motivated will only add value to your small business.

After reading the strategies of how you can add value to your small business, what have you learned?

What ways do you add value to your employees and/or helpers?

How can you add value to your employees and/or helpers using creative techniques?

Think about it!

Now let's see how you can add value to your products.

ADD VALUE TO YOUR PRODUCTS

When I think of ways to add value to my small business, I think about what type of products I can sell to help someone. I think of how I can bundle my products to add value to the products I sell. I think of how my customers can leave my store happy because of the quality products that were sold to them.

☞ CREATE BUNDLE PACKAGES

I add value to my products by creating bundle packages by selling items as buy-one-get-one-free.

You can add value to your products by _____.

You can add value to your products by _____.

You can add value to your products by _____.

ADDING VALUE TAKES TIME

Adding value to the products you sell may take time. I don't believe this is an overnight process; however, as you continue to grow your business, you will notice what products sell and what products don't sell and why.

You will learn how to continue to look for ways to add value to your products.

How do you plan to add value to your products? Are you going to add value to your products by using one of the strategies I use?

Do you have a strategy of your own you may want use?

While adding value to your products is important, let's not forget to add value to your services. It fits in the same category.

ADD VALUE TO YOUR SERVICES

When I think of ways to add value to my small business, I think about what type of services I can sell to help someone. I think of how I can make things a little bit easier for others. Sometimes you may think your customers understand most of the things you explain to them; however, this is not always true. It's your job to offer services to help the customers who may need the extra help. As a shopper, I like to shop at stores that add value services to help make my shopping experience the best every time I frequent the business.

Example 1:

Offer a one month free trial of a service.

Example 2:

Offer a free workshop to explain how to use a service.

Example 3:

Offer free resources about a service.

Keep thinking… now how do you plan to add value to your services?

Make a list. Then work on practicing adding value to your services you offer.

You can add value to your services by _____.

You can add value to your services by _____.

You can add value to your services by _____.

Fantastic! You have brainstormed ways you add value to your services. Now let's look at ways you can add value to your suppliers and vendors.

ADD VALUE TO YOUR SUPPLIERS AND VENDORS

Do you need to add value to your suppliers and vendors? You can't go wrong with helping your suppliers grow their business too. You can do this by ordering products from multiple vendors.

Dividing your orders gives you an opportunity to help increase the sales of all suppliers and vendors who help you stay in business. Share the orders.

Thank your suppliers and vendors for helping you choose the best reliable products to offer at your place of business. When my suppliers and vendors tell me something to help benefit my business, I always thank them for their advice. Thanking your suppliers and vendors will help you build valuable relationships. If a vendor is having a huge sale, you may be the first small business they call to take advantage of the opportunity. I have experienced this several times. Track your packages instead of calling in to have suppliers and vendors to constantly track packages. Technology is so convenient for small business owners. Tracking your packages frees up some time for your suppliers and/or vendors to focus on selling. The small things really count.

Think of ways you can add value to your suppliers and vendors. How can you make their job easier? Don't forget to say thank you!

Up next, how can you add value to the people who provide services to your business? Let's see!

ADD VALUE TO THE PEOPLE WHO PROVIDE SERVICES TO YOUR BUSINESS

☞ MAIL CARRIERS

Mail carriers' jobs can be challenging. I greet them with a smile, honk my horn at them to say hi when I see them out in the town, or have boxes of chocolate for them during the holidays, or a cold soda on hot days during the summer months.

Your products may travel a long ways to get to you, so don't forget about the people who have helped get products to you. Always be appreciative. I feel really special when I know my mail carriers go the extra mile to deliver my packages hours before the scheduled delivery time.

I believe when you help others, you may receive help in return.

☞ WEBSITE DESIGNERS

While I am tech savvy, when it comes to getting help to build websites and learning how to use search engine optimization to increase my online presence, I ask my wonderful website designers.

So you should add value to the service provider who designs your website. You can add value to them by sending them referrals.

☞ MENTORS

Mentors pour out their knowledge and time to help your dreams become a reality, so don't forget to let them know how much they are appreciated. Send an electronic thank-you card on social media or send a surprise bonus for their hard work. As a mentor myself, I understand how much time and effort is put into helping others.

Now that you see why it's important to add value to the people who provide services to your small business, let's look at how you can add value to people you meet in the market, whether they are your customers or not, because eventually they may become a customer.

ADD VALUE TO PEOPLE YOU MEET IN THE MARKET

☞ SMILE, SAY HI, AND OPEN A DOOR

When it's hot outside I like to walk downtown and meet people. Some I know and some I don't know. It seems like most people I run into know me, but whether I know them or not, I smile, say hi, or open a door for them. I don't think you can go wrong being kind to others.

THE PERSON MAY ALREADY BE A CUSTOMER

While I was at the local drugstore shopping, I bumped into one of my customers who asked when will my book about how to grow a small business be published. While I know I was not on the clock (as a small business owner I don't think business

owners are ever off the clock), I chatted with him and answered his questions and he was thankful for my time and left smiling.

To know that he is eagerly awaiting the release of my book, and to hear this from a person I have only been in contact with three times, inspired me to continue to build relationships with my customers because you never know who you can help with your experience and knowledge.

Do you see your customers out in the market? What do you do?

*Snap! *Snap! *Snap!
Watch out, here comes ...
The Paparazzi

As you continue to grow your business, you will become more popular and people you don't know will know your name and call you by name while you are out in the market shopping. This may be in your hometown where your business is located, or maybe in other towns far away. If you offer quality products and services and provide excellent customer service, people will find you. Everybody shopping in a particular store might know you and feel like they need to ask you questions. Always be kind to your customers no matter where you see them.

ADD VALUE TO PEOPLE WHO HELP YOU STAY IN BUSINESS

People who help you stay in business can be friends you talk to on a daily basis. I tend to have a lot of friends who are small business owners, which is a good thing because we are always bouncing ideas off each other and finding ways to add value to continue to help each other grow personally or to grow each other's businesses.

You can do this by buying your friend books that relate to their business so they can learn something new.

You can do this by volunteering to help your friend (small business owner) with a task such as cleaning or answering phone calls.

You can do this by inviting the people who help you stay in business out to lunch or dinner, or even to grab a cup of coffee.

How do you plan to add value to the people who help you stay in business? Have you thought about this?

ADD VALUE TO THE BUSINESS ENVIRONMENT

Make your customers feel like they are at home. When they walk into your place of business, your customers should feel welcome and your business environment should relax them.

TOMEKA PRESCOTT

Adding value to your business is important because you want to continue to be a successful business owner who is able to continue to grow a business while helping others. I think about how I can make my business a fun place for consumers to shop. I don't just envision how I would like the shopping environment to feel like. I ask my customers what they would like to see in my store to make their shopping experience more enjoyable. I ensure that the shopping environment is friendly, safe, and warm.

This is one way I add value to my business.

I use what I have to grow my business: space, money, products, and services. I don't worry about what I don't have. As my business grows, I have noticed that I usually have what I need and I work on adding value to the business environment on a daily basis.

Adding value to your business will be a key to growing your small business.

It will be a key to differentiating your business from your competitors. And a key to creating a business of VALUE!

SUMMARY

Okay, back to wrapping things up. It is very important for you to add value to your small business. Work on adding value daily. Create an environment that fosters adding value to others. Hopefully, the strategies and tips I have written about in this chapter will help you continue to grow your business so you can gain that competitive advantage in your industry and keep it!

IF YOU DO NOTHING ELSE AFTER READING THIS CHAPTER

I want you to write a paragraph or two of how you plan to add value to your small business.

You can share your success stories with me at:

www.TomekaPrescott.com

Now that you have written your paragraph(s), join me in Chapter 8 where you will learn why branding is important and how to create branding for your small business.

BRANDING YOUR BUSINESS

As a small business owner, you can brand yourself and your business to stand out in the market. You should work on branding your business daily to gain a competitive edge in your industry. Once you have branded your business, don't stop there. Continue to grow your brand identity for the life of your small business.

TOMEKA PRESCOTT

WHAT I THINK ABOUT BRANDING

Have you ever tried to recall the name of a store you've shopped at or a person you've conducted business with?

Well I have. It's hard to remember names of businesses that are not well-branded. I forget. Better yet, some small businesses do not have a logo.

You want customers to know who you are in your market, what you sell, and how you can deliver your products and services to meet their needs and wants. But how do you do this? How do you stand out like companies such as major retail chain stores and service businesses?

You may already have good branding strategies in place to grow your business. However, I want to share with you what I know from personal experience about branding a small business from the bottom up.

In Chapter 6, I have shared with you what happened in the market of São Paulo, Brazil, so you already know you have to do something different to stand out! Let's look closer at branding.

BRANDING IS NOT AN OVERNIGHT PROCESS

My sister says, "You will only get as far as you allow yourself to go. If you don't believe in YOU then no one else will. The more time you invest in yourself and your brand in the beginning, the less time you will need to invest later."

It takes time to brand a small business. You may be thinking, how much time? I will share how long it took my family to brand a small business. I will also share what I know from experience from working at my family's small business that started from the bottom.

Branding the small business was not an easy task.

> It took ensuring that we answered every single phone call saying thank you for calling (business name) or (business name) how may I help you?
> It took continuing to correct customers when they simply called the business other names such as the cellphone store.
> It took not leaving our business name and number off a marketing flyer.

DON'T CONFUSE CUSTOMERS WITH AN EXTRAVAGANT BUSINESS NAME

Make your business name relevant and simple. You want to create a business name that is easy for customers to remember. Customers should be able to say your business name correctly the first time. They should not have to put a lot of thought into saying your name correctly or remembering where they are shopping.

Which Name Can You Remember?

Fun Cakes and More Plus Sweet Candy Hearts and Candy Tarts

Or

Fun Cakes and Candy

This is just an example.

PUT YOUR NAME ON EVERYTHING

I mailed out postcards with our name at the very top of the card in BOLD WRITING. I continue to use this technique to get my name out in the market. Once consumers continue to see your name on promotional items, such as shopping bags and t-shirts, they will learn your business name.

Don't forget to add your business number too. Always do this; don't just include this information on some items, but not others. Include this information on as many promotional items as possible, such as:

➢ Shopping Bags
➢ Pens
➢ Packaging
➢ T-shirts
➢ Balloons

If you do it right, you'll eventually hear people say they heard about your business because they saw your stylus writing pen in the market. When my sister came to me one day and said, "Tomeka, your business stylus pens (with my business name and logo) were used at the sign-up table for a field day event held in town," I knew the branding strategy was bringing good results.

Don't just include your business name, logo, and phone number, you should also include the website of your business on marketing materials.

YOU DON'T HAVE TO USE A LOT OF ADVERTISEMENT OUTLETS

Word-of-mouth and postcard advertisements were used to brand the family's business to get started.

Actually, most of the advertising was done through word-of-mouth advertising. I have touched on the importance of word-of-mouth advertising in Chapter 3.

We verbally told customers the name of the business, and pointed at the business sign saying who we are and what we do.

IT TOOK FIVE YEARS

It took doing all of this during the first five years of being in business, and after the first five years, we continued doing the same thing to continue to grow the brand in the market.

We've never stopped branding the business.

The same strategies used since day one are currently being used for the life of the small business. I told you that you don't have to make things complicated in business. If strategies work, don't stop using them for the life of your business.

To keep up with my branding strategies you can view my page at: www.TomekaPrescott.com

Now that you know how long it took my family to brand a small business...

BE CAREFUL NOT TO BRAND A SUPPLIER OR CONTRACTOR BUSINESS

Branding does not have to be difficult. Work hard to build your own brand. Be yourself!

TOMEKA PRESCOTT

If you choose to represent several other businesses as an authorized dealer, don't make the mistake of branding the suppliers' business instead of your business. Customers can easily get this mixed up.

Some companies may send you their bags and promotional items to use, and while this is good, it may confuse the customer. This is what you don't want to do.

You want your customers to know your business name and your name. So always use your bags and your promotional items to brand your small business.

Now that I have told you my personal story about what I've learned about branding, let's dig deeper and see what you'll learn in Chapter 8.

BRANDING YOUR SMALL BUSINESS

This chapter is about branding your business for growth. You will learn why branding is important and learn strategies and techniques for branding your small business. You will also have the opportunity to create your own branding strategies. You will explore how to get noticed in your market, leave a positive

image, build loyal customers who love your brand, and connect with customers through your brand.

In the previous chapter, you've learned how to add value to your business. Now you will learn how to brand your business in practical steps.

BRANDING IS IMPORTANT BECAUSE...

You can tell people who you are through branding.

Now let's look at two things you want to get out of branding.

GET NOTICED IN YOUR MARKET

In our market today, technology is continuing to change the way small business owners brand their business. However, you don't need to hide behind technology because branding your business is more than people knowing who you are online. In fact, branding goes far beyond your online presence. As a small business owner, you want to be noticed in the offline market too. Use branding strategies from back-in-the days, and mix them with current branding strategies.

Many people in a local community might not know about the new service you've launched because you didn't send out postcards or mail-outs. This is a good way to get your name built in your local community.

Let's get down and take it back to the basics.

Knock down the Internet walls and physically get out in your local market to brand yourself and your small business.

You have what it takes to get the job done.

LEAVE A POSITIVE IMAGE

When you effectively brand your small business, consumers should remember who you are and what you sell. So your goal here is to leave a positive image in the market. I have written about several strategies you can use to increase value in your market, which will then increase your brand. You want your customers to know that when they see your logo or business name, they can get help and receive great services and products.

You want consumers to see your logo or business name and know what they can buy and what type of service your small business offers. Your goal is to offer the best products and services possible so when a consumer is in the market looking for an item or service you sell, they'll think about you and only you and then stop by at your small business.

IF ONE BRANDING TECHNIQUE DOESN'T WORK

Don't worry. You can build your brand. Don't give up. It can be done; just keep using different techniques to brand your business. You'll never know what may work or what may not work if you don't go for it.

Have you mapped out your plan to create a positive image in your target market?

This is what I do to create a positive image in the market.

BUILD LOYAL CUSTOMERS WHO LOVE MY BRAND

Your goal and focus point is to build a loyal customer base that loves your brand and promotes your brand to their friends and family members. Simply because they love your brand, they love who you are and what you do to help them and others. Your loyal customers will even advertise your business via word-of-mouth for you. Some may bring customers to your place of business and help match them up with products and services they currently use.

I see this happen frequently.

How do you plan to build loyal customers who love your brand?

I CONNECT WITH MY CUSTOMERS THROUGH MY BRAND

Being able to relate with a customer through your brand is very important. You want to make a positive relationship connection with your customers. Think about the favorite stores where you like to shop and tell me what you think about their brand.

HOW DO YOU CONNECT WITH THE BRAND OF YOUR FAVORITE STORES?

How do you connect with the brands of the products and services that are offered at your favorite stores?

I am a type of person who wants to buy a quality product and/or receive quality services. I will drive the extra mile for these types of products and services. The hour drive to get there doesn't bother me at all.

How will you connect with your customers through your brand?

1.
2.
3.

I DON'T STOP GROWING MY BRAND IDENTITY

Know that I will always continue to grow my brand because I know that businesses grow through branding.

TOMEKA PRESCOTT

Let's say you are a professional and want to grow your brand identity in your market. Growing your brand identity in a market can be tough; however, stay focused. YOU, the small business owner, are the brand identity of your business. When you are working with your clients do what you say you are going to do each and every time you come in contact with clients and/or customers.

You will continuously build trust with your clients and they will come back to conduct business with you.

YES, I PACKAGE MY BRAND!

Your brand will speak for you. Start small and be creative. You may even want to find something big companies are doing and put your own twist to it when creating your packaging. Your quality packaging will help create your brand. Sooner or later, it will pay off. Your goal is for consumers to recognize your packaging in the market, and when they need your products and services, they will remember your name and shop at your business, or buy your products and services.

HOW TO BRAND YOUR BUSINESS IN PRACTICAL STEPS

FIRST, USE SOCIAL MEDIA TO BRAND YOUR BUSINESS

I use social media to brand my small business, but as I've explained earlier, I don't hide behind the Internet walls. It is important to create a social media plan to brand your business

because you'll want to keep up with implementing different ways to use technology to grow your business.

At first, I thought, well I have been in business for a long time, so I really don't need to use social media to advertise my business. Then I came up with a lot of excuses why I did not want to use social media until one day I decided to advertise my business through social media.

Since I've started using social media as a way to promote my small business, I've seen sales increase. Also, through using social media to brand my small business, I was able to tap into new markets and meet new people. I have gained new customers and have had great success with marketing my community service events online. Using social media to brand your small business is important because it's an easy way to be seen by potential customers all over the world. In addition, membership in some social media websites is free.

Your goal is to build a lot of followers.

Are you following me on all of my social media sites yet? If not, visit my website at:

www.TomekaPrescott.com

Have fun following me.

Be social online. I use several social media websites to market my business. I have a presence on these sites so people can keep up with my latest products and services. I didn't create the social media pages just to sit back and watch the likes; I keep my page current with up-to-date information of the latest specials. This is a great way to get your local community involved with what's going on at your place of business.

Stay in touch. I will continue to update my social media pages.

Now there are some more social media websites I have plans to use in the future. It's always good to stay abreast to what's going in the market and tag along so you don't get left behind—only if it's a good fit for your business.

No one wants to be left behind. Technology is changing the way we do things fast - very fast. So don't be afraid to try using different social media sites to brand your business. There are benefits of using several social media sites to brand your business.

CRAFT A SOCIAL MEDIA PLAN

Do you plan on creating a social media plan to grow and market your business?

A plan that you'll write down on paper and implement?

If yes, let's start planning now.

One simple tip is to survey your customers to see what social media sites they are using. Once you have gathered the data, you can chart things out and join the social media sites where your customers are socializing.

What social media websites do you plan to add to your current social media strategy and why?

1.
2.
3.
4.
5.

How do you plan to attract followers to your social pages to continue to grow your list of followers?

YOU CAN...

➤ Add your social media site names to your business cards.
➤ Offer a discount to your clients if they follow you.
➤ Verbally ask your clients to join your network of social media sites.

What's your personal strategy? Use this space to write your strategy.

SECOND, THINK OF ALTERNATE WAYS TO BRAND YOUR BUSINESS. CONTINUE TO USE YOUR CURRENT BRANDING STRATEGY BUT ALSO DO SOMETHING UNIQUE THAT YOU'VE NEVER DONE BEFORE.

When you think of alternate ways to brand your business, you are on the right path to creating a brand that will help grow your business. Now we are going to add more branding strategies to the current strategies you are using.

This may be something small or big. I've had success with implementing different branding strategies.

- ➤ Create social media business cards to pass out to your customers and/or clients to brand your business.
- ➤ Turn your print business card into an electronic business card. When you send an email to someone, include your business card on the email signature line to brand your business.
- ➤ Start a billboard campaign with the information from your flyers and brochures to brand your business.
- ➤ Create and post a video on your webpage that describes a new product or service you are selling.

Think of alternate ways you can brand your business.

I currently use_____to brand my business.

I will implement this _____.

I currently use _____to brand my business.

I will implement this _____.

I currently use _____to brand my business.

I will implement this _____.

I currently use _____to brand my business.

I will implement this _____.

This is just a start, but now let's look at why it's good to take inventory of what works and what does not work when branding your small business. This is important because you don't want to waste time with branding strategies that are not effective. You

can spend the extra time on growing other parts of your small business instead.

THIRD, TAKE INVENTORY OF WHAT WORKS AND WHAT DOES NOT WORK. IT WOULDN'T BE GOOD TO CONTINUE TO USE A STRATEGY THAT DOES NOT WORK FOR YOUR SMALL BUSINESS.

You may know that all businesses do not grow because they use the same branding strategies.

It takes using current strategies that have been effective for your small business as well as implementing new strategies. Create a list and monitor each strategy success to see what works and what does not work. I do this by asking my customers how they heard about my small business, then keep a running tally.

For example if a customer indicates they heard about your business via a social media website you may want to make note of this so you can see what branding strategy is most effective for your small business. When you find out what works best for your small business keep doing it—over and over again!

HOW DID YOU HEAR ABOUT ME?

Social Media XXXXXXXXXXXXXXXXXXXXXXXXX

Word-of-Mouth XXXXXXXXXX

Flyer XXXXXXXXX

Shopping Bag XXXXXXX

Billboard XXX

Do this on a daily or weekly basis; don't worry you don't have to ask all your customers or clients how they heard about you, but

as you think about it ask them. At the end of each month, total up your "How did you hear about me?" marks. Then create a chart so you can see a visual picture.

How Did You Hear About Me Results Chart

FOURTH, BRAND YOUR BUSINESS SLOWLY. IT TAKES TIME— THERE IS NO NEED TO RUSH THIS STEP

Branding your business should be a learning process. You don't have to rush the branding process. Take this process slowly. Branding any small business takes time.

Keep putting your brand out in the market.

Keep helping your customers the best you can.

Keep providing great customer service.

Keep building relationships with your customers.

Don't give in or give up on branding your small business. Remember, do it over and over again, and don't forget to ask others to help you brand your business.

Fifth, Know When To Rebrand Your Business—You Should "Refresh" Your Brand If You Need To

Once you've begun to use different strategies to brand your business, you'll love coming up with more strategies. While it's important to know how to use the different branding strategies, it's also important to know when to rebrand your business. I call this refreshing your brand. I want you to...

> ➤ Stay current and up-to-date with what's going on in the market.
> ➤ Stand out in the market and gain a competitive advantage and to continue to compete with the larger businesses.
> ➤ Do something different to help create business growth for your small business.

I did this by updating my logo to create a fresher look.

Make branding fun; implement branding strategies on a daily basis. Most importantly know that your products and services are valuable and stand behind your brand to grow your small business.

SUMMARY

Continue to brand your small business every day to gain a competitive edge in your market. Branding takes time so don't rush this process. Also, focus on branding your name and your business name too. When you have branded your name and your business name you are on your way to growing your small business. Don't give up.

AFTER READING ABOUT BRANDING IF YOU DO NOTHING ELSE I WANT YOU TO...

Do one thing to brand your business that you have not done before. For my small business, this one thing is to reach out to Circle D Designs to have them design a bag for the packaging of this book.

I am thankful to have Circle D Designs to take on branding projects. Each and every time success is delivered.

> *You can have a professional help you in the designing process; you can create a brand that will last forever. I know because I did this.*
>
> TOMEKA PRESCOTT

Now that you are on the road to becoming well-branded, let's go forward to Chapter 9 where you will learn why back-up plans are important.

SECTION FIVE

Sustaining Your Business

Chapter 9

CREATE BACK-UP PLANS

WEATHER THE STORMS

Anchor your small business.

TOMEKA PRESCOTT

As a small business owner, you are tasked to handle a lot of things. You have to help customers, place orders, and control departments. While you're doing all of these things, you have to also prepare for the unexpected, such as knowing what to do when you can't open your business.

Have a plan in place to know what you are going to do when the unexpected happens, so you can continue to stay in business to

serve your community. Even though things may be going on around you, don't move, or take your eyes off your mission and vision. How are you going to prepare for the unexpected?

LEARNING HOW TO PREPARE FOR THE UNEXPECTED

When you have back-up plans in place, you are on your way to growing your small business. Continue to prepare yourself in business.

TOMEKA PRESCOTT

This chapter is about creating back-up plans while growing your business. You will explore the back-up plans I have created in business and create your very own back-up plans to use in your small business.

You will learn why back-up plans are important and learn what type of back-up plans you'll need to create. You will also learn how to implement back-up plans to help you avoid business failure.

Now let's see why back-up plans are important. In this chapter I will discuss four back-up plans that you may want to create and how I implement each plan in my small business.

THE IMPORTANCE OF CREATING BACK-UP PLANS

Creating back-up plans are important because you never know

when your business sales will slow down; you never know when you may have to step away from the business to take care of a personal issue; you will never know when your technology may crash; and you may never know when the market may change or the weather may cause a physical business to close temporarily.

Have back-up plans ready to use in case of any emergency. As you continue to grow your small business, you'll learn the type of back-up plan you'll need and how to create your back-up plans to fit your personal small business. Not all businesses are the same, so your back-up plans may be different from my small business back-up plans.

Back-up plans are easy to create; they should be easy to implement and revise. When you start to think about what you're going to include in your back-up plans, avoid making your back-up plans difficult.

Anyone should be able to read, understand, and implement your back-up plans because you're not going to be the only one to use the back-up plans.

HOW TO CREATE BACK-UP PLANS FOR YOUR SMALL BUSINESS

CREATE A WEATHER BACK-UP PLAN

I've experienced two ice/snow storms and heard about an earthquake that took place in the state where I live. These events were unexpected.

I wasn't able to open my small business a couple of days during the snowy weather. The roads were too icy and it was cold.

Where I am from, people don't venture out much to shop in this kind of weather. Most of the stores close so if people wanted to go out to shop, they wouldn't have many options to choose from.

I am able to still operate my business when things like this happen because I prepare for days like these by saving money in advance.

When you are a small business owner and you operate your business day-by-day without saving money, you may notice a financial impact when the unexpected happens. No one wants to have their business affected.

You can avoid this through saving money. If you don't have money saved, you can refer back to Chapter 3 to gain some insights about different strategies to earn extra money to grow your small business.

As I've indicated before, you should have fun while growing your small business; you don't want to worry about not having a back-up plan in place when storms hit.

In business, there are some things that you can't control; therefore, you would want to create back-up plans so you can continue to operate your small business smoothly during uncontrollable situations.

There are many different types of storms that can affect the operation of your small business. Here is a list of some storms that I've experienced while in business.

- Rain storm
- Snow storm
- Thunderstorm
- Ice storm

During storms like these, business slows down drastically.

For example, on a rainy day I may only see 10 customers instead of the normal 25.

WHAT I DO WHEN THERE ARE STORMS

If the storm is minor, like a rain storm, I use these days to get organized, or simply take a break and prepare for the next business day.

If the storm is major, such as a snow storm, I work from home. In my home office I have a desk, laptop, and a wireless internet device. I forward my business phone calls to my cellular phone so I am still able to take important phone calls and help customers with their purchases. If customers would like to shop, I direct them to my online store so they can purchase the products and services they want or need.

From home, I am able to operate my business without skipping a beat. This has allowed me to continue to operate my small business when storms happens.

Think about how you can prepare for the unexpected.

_____

_____

_____

Organize your workspace at home to get ready to work at home when the unexpected happens. Have a system in place to make

the transition smooth.

CREATE A TECHNOLOGY BACK-UP PLAN

Technology is fun to use. You can automate business tasks to make keeping up with business a bit easier, but what if your technology devices crash? What would you do?

TOMEKA PRESCOTT

I took an electronic class in high school.

I played with motherboards. I had no clue what I was doing. I am now using what I've learned in that one class in high school at my place of business.

Working in the electronics industry, I learned that when it comes to using technology in the workplace, you have to have back-up plans because there's going to be a day when your technology may not work.

I work in the electronics industry at least five days per week. I became tech savvy.

I can fix cellular phones, disassemble and assemble. I had to build upon my technology skills daily to learn the ins and outs. If you have little knowledge in IT, troubleshooting a computer, or trying to recover a document you've lost on the computer don't worry, because you can get help.

That's why it's important to have an effective technology back-up plan in place.

UNABLE TO REGISTER A NEW CLIENT VIA TECHNOLOGY?

What would you do if you were unable to register a new client into the computer system?

As you continue to grow your small business, you'll need to keep up with each client. You can do this by registering each customer into a customer database as you conduct business with them for the first time. Let's say that your internet stops working as you're registering a customer. What would you do? Think about this as I share with you what I do when I'm unable to use technology at my place of business.

DAMAGED COMPUTER?

There was a time when I created a name and address database list of over 2000 customers. This complete database was typed into a spreadsheet document. These were customers' names and addresses that I've collected over a few years. Then one day my computer decided it wanted to crash. I wanted to cry but I didn't. I had to hold back the tears and push forward.

How did I push forward? I bought a new computer. This time I didn't store my database in a spreadsheet. Instead I used an online marketing database website to store my list of names and addresses. This approach worked because I've used the same online marketing database for at least 10 years.

Also, there have been times when I've saved all of my flyers to advertise my business in a document on the computer, the computer crashed, and I no longer had access to my flyers. Now, I use online file storage sites to store files. This has helped

because I am able to retrieve my documents from any computer as long as I have Internet connection.

Create a technology back-up plan so when things happen you can continue to operate your business smoothly. In your technology back-up plan, include information such as who will fix your computer if it breaks, and how you would back up the information using an external storage.

Using an external storage is a great way to avoid losing your important information. External storages can be purchased at office supply stores.

INTERNET DOWN?

If you process your credit card payments online, or via your cellular phone, or tablet, have a plan in place if the Internet goes down. What would you do if you are in the middle of a sale and don't have access to the Internet to complete the payment?

This is what I do.

I'll ask the customer if it's possible to pay with cash. This is the only other option I offer my customers. My customers usually don't make a big deal of this. Your goal will be to operate your business as smoothly as possible. You can do this by having back-up plans in place.

With technology being so popular in the business industry, always have technology back-up plans. Think about what you would do if you're unable to connect to the Internet to operate your small business.

You can always consider taking the manual route if you don't have access to technology.

WHAT WOULD YOU DO?

Would you buy an external storage hard drive to back up your documents?

Would you save your documents in a storage cloud?

Would you ask your friend who is tech savvy to help you create a technology back-up plan?

CREATE A PERSONAL AND EMPLOYEE EMERGENCY BACK-UP PLAN

Create a back-up-plan for emergencies. If you're not feeling well one day, you'll already know how you can step away while the business continues to be operated.

Personally, I have some days where I do not feel like working. During these days, I stay at home. I am able to do this because I have created a back-up plan for emergencies.

If a family emergency or any type of emergency arises, an emergency plan is great because it may be difficult to close your doors for long periods of times.

WHAT CAN YOU DO WHEN YOU NEED TO STEP AWAY?

There may be some days you need to step away from your small business. Since you are a small business owner, it doesn't mean that you always have to run the show.

You can take a break.

TOMEKA PRESCOTT

You can train your employees on what to do when you need to step away from your small business. Once you train employees, you can have a sense of ease when life happens because you'll know that the business can continue to operate.

You can have a list created of your normal day-to-day tasks for the employees. It would be a good idea to have a key employee step in to help you.

EMPLOYEE EMERGENCIES

If your employees are not able to come to work, you don't have to close your doors. You can step in to operate the business to complete their job tasks.

If you decide to have employees, it will be very important for you to train more than one key employee.

The next back-up plan is extremely important because I've seen businesses close their doors without warning.

CREATE A SUPPLIER AND VENDOR BACK-UP PLAN

Vendors and suppliers may go out of business overnight without a warning.

TOMEKA PRESCOTT

Have a backup plan just in case one of your main vendors or suppliers goes out of business overnight via a closing, merger, or sale. Over the years that I have been in business, I have had major vendors close their doors…and some only gave a day's notice of their closing. When company A closed, I had to use company B to continue to operate my small business. If I didn't have company B in place as a back-up, I would have lost a lot of sales.

HAVE MORE THAN ONE VENDOR AND SUPPLIER

It is also good to have multiple vendors just in case one vendor is low or out of stock on the items you need fast…especially during the peak season and the holidays.

For example, let's say you're the owner of a service-based business. Instead of having one vendor to supply your equipment, have multiple vendors. Prices may be lower with vendor number 2 than vendor number 1. Having more than one vendor or supplier is just another way to be creative in business.

You would not have to spend countless hours researching to find a new vendor and then build a relationship with them. You will already have back-up vendors that you currently do business with.

Supporting multiple vendors can also add more value to your business because you are helping more than one small business grow as you conduct business with them. Can you recall Chapter 7 about adding value to others?

To get started, list your vendors and suppliers here.

- _____
- _____
- _____
- _____
- _____

Here is an inside tip to dealing with calls from suppliers and vendors.

OVERLOAD ON CALLS FROM SUPPLIERS AND VENDORS

I had to create a plan to handle these calls. This is what I do. As soon as calls come in from vendors and suppliers that I am not currently working with, I answer the phone and simply ask the vendors and/or suppliers to send me an email with product, promotion, or sales information. I have a set time throughout the day to check emails to see if I am interested in conducting business with the suppliers and/or vendors. I look into what the vendors and suppliers have to offer because I'll never know if they have what I am looking for to grow my business if I don't take the time to see what they have to offer.

However, using the information I mentioned above saves me a lot of time, and frees up my business line. As a small business owner, you may be the only worker growing your business so you need all the time and energy you can get to stay focused on your business.

SUMMARY

Back-up plans in business are important to create. If you don't create back-up plans you may have a hard time operating your business smoothly. You should get into the habit of creating back-up plans. Once you've created your list of back-up plans, be ready to update your back-up plans when needed. I usually revise my back-up plans at least once per year. If I need to change something, I change it; if the back-up plan works, I don't change anything. Next you'll work on creating at least one back-up plan.

To download a sample of one of my back-up plans you can go to: www.TomekaPrescott.com

IF YOU DO AT LEAST ONE THING AFTER READING THIS CHAPTER.

Create at least one back-up plan for your business.

You can start by creating a weather back-up plan. Then you can work on creating the other back-up plans. Figure out what you're going to do to continue operating your business during a storm.

Now let's go forward to Chapter 10 where we'll learn how to control inventory and watch your bottom line.

WATCH YOUR BOTTOM LINE AND CONTROL INVENTORY

Start growing your business on the right foot. Watch and monitor your bottom line and control inventory.

TOMEKA PRESCOTT

Watching your bottom line and controlling inventory is a hit or a miss for small business owners. You can start to think about how you will watch and monitor your bottom line and can create your inventory plan of how to control inventory at your small business. You should monitor your cash flow on a daily

basis and avoid overbuying equipment and products you don't need. Overbuying is an easy mistake to make.

WHAT IS WATCHING YOUR BOTTOM LINE AND CONTROLLING INVENTORY ALL ABOUT?

You will explore strategies to help you strengthen your bottom line and to help you control inventory. You will also learn why watching your bottom line is important when growing your business and how to watch your bottom line in practical steps.

You will learn why it's important to control inventory as a small business owner and you'll learn different strategies you can implement to help with controlling inventory.

As you explore this chapter, take notes of what kind of inventory you carry in your business. Make an inventory list of products, services, equipment, and supplies. I operate a retail electronics store and I will share my experience with ordering products that I sell in my store.

WATCHING YOUR BOTTOM LINE IS IMPORTANT

Some small business owners may fret about watching their bottom line. You may go day-to-day looking for ways to save money and looking for ways to build a cushion to strengthen your bottom line. So many small businesses go out of business because their bottom line is not watched and not continually being strengthened. Just because another business is able to have success in selling a particular product or service does not mean

the business down the road may have success selling the same products and/or services.

Small business owners can't think they are going to thrive and blossom because competitors or other businesses are touching the stars. Blooming overnight isn't the strategy small business owners should focus on because it takes time to grow a business.

WATCH YOUR BOTTOM LINE DAILY

> *As you continue to grow your business, watch your bottom line daily.*
>
> TOMEKA PRESCOTT

Practice watching your bottom line daily.

It is important to watch your bottom line in business because there will be days where you may be unable to operate your business. For example, there may be times when you experience inclement weather such as snow and ice storms and are unable to open your small business.

I have mentioned this in Chapter 9.

Watching your bottom line is also important because you don't want all of the money you make going towards paying business expenses only. So that's why you need to keep business expenses as low as possible.

You can do it!

HOW TO WATCH YOUR BOTTOM LINE

Your goal here is to keep your business expenses as low as possible so you can make a profit in business when you sell your products and services to your customers. It wouldn't be fun to always have to take most of your money to pay basic operation bills. You don't have to pay $150.00 for phone services when you can pay $55.00 per month. You should always look for ways to reduce the amount of a bill.

This includes:

- Power
- Phone
- Internet
- Cable

Your goal will be to get low service from the start. Once you watch and monitor your monthly bills, start looking at other things to watch and monitor such as…

AVOID PAYING TOO MUCH SHIPPING AND FREIGHT CHARGES

When ordering products and/or services, you may incur shipping and freight charges. Some vendors and suppliers may offer you free shipping, but what if they don't? Watch your invoices to see how you can create a plan to save on these charges. I simply ask my suppliers—can I receive free shipping?

I usually get a yes if I order a set minimum amount of products. I like to hear the yes, because I am able to save the cash that I would have spent on shipping and freight. This is something I am still working on improving every time I place orders.

Avoid Buying Things You Simply Don't Need

Some small business owners may have the urge to buy things that they don't need. If you have the extra cash flow, you don't have to spend it on things you don't really need to grow your business.

Avoid buying unnecessary items. Ask yourself if the item you're considering will help you grow your business. If yes, have a plan for using the products for business growth. If not, then it's probably not a good idea to buy it.

Build A Cash Cushion In Your Savings Account

Build a cash cushion in your business savings account for emergencies. You may want to use one of the strategies I've discussed in Chapter 3 to build a cash cushion. I've also touched on this in Chapter 9. Do what you can with what you have to build the cash cushion you're going to need.

Strengthen Cash Flow

Know how much money is coming in your business and how much money is going out. Small business owners should always use strategies to strengthen the cash flow. If you are spending 10,000.00 per month and generating 12,000.00 per month, which leaves you with a profit of 2,000.00 per month, know what you're doing with the 2,000.00. Generating a profit for your business does not mean that you're able to increase your business profitability.

One way I strengthen cash flow is by monitoring the commissions percentages I receive from each vendor or supplier. Sometimes it's only a 2% difference, but this adds up

in the long run. When I see that I am able to earn a higher percentage commission rate from a vendor, I conduct business with the vendor that's going to offer me the highest amount. Over time, this has helped me strengthen my bottom line.

Think of strategies you can use to strengthen the cash flow of your small business.

Strengthen cash flow _____

Strengthen cash flow _____

Strengthen cash flow _____

> *Now that you are watching your bottom line,*
> *let's anchor down controlling inventory.*
>
> Tomeka Prescott

WHY IS CONTROLLING INVENTORY IMPORTANT?

As a small business owner, I had to learn how to control inventory. I would overstock on items that would not sell and I didn't have an inventory plan in place. If I've ordered too much of an item that was outdated I simply would bag it up and put it in storage. Putting items in storage does not increase profitability.

Yes, most of my overstock items went to storage.

Why would you want to store items you've overstocked and can't sell or use?

Why not simply create a plan to control inventory so you can avoid this from happening?

Implement a plan to control inventory.

If you feel like you've tried to control inventory and have not been successful with this, we'll discuss outsourcing departments and how you can get people to help you with difficult tasks that are not your specialty.

When you are able to control inventory, you are able to create cash flow.

When inventory is controlled you'll avoid overstocking products, equipment, and supplies used to operate your business. Allowing more room to increase your cash flow will help grow your business.

CREATE AN INVENTORY LIST

As your business grows your inventory will change as the market changes and grows as well. I like to create an inventory list of the products and services I sell so I can see what I have to offer my customers. Creating an inventory list allows me to categorize the products and services I sell.

When I create my orders, I order from my inventory list of products and services so as I am ordering, I can ensure that I am ordering a variety of items to sell. If I am testing the market with a new product, I will purchase less than five products and see how they sell. If the products sell in the market, I will order more. If they don't sell, I buy and test other products in the market. If you have employees, let them help you out with this process.

As a small business owner, I am not always working at my store, so I tend to miss what customers ask for or want. This is where employees can help you continue to listen to your customers so you can order the products and services they need. Ask your employees or helpers to write things down on note pads or pre-

order sheets when customers ask for a particular product or service. Also, don't forget to record a contact name and number for the customer so you can follow-up.

Creating an inventory list should help jump start learning how to control inventory.

Test the market.

If products and services are not selling, don't buy them. If they are selling, you can estimate how many you can keep in your inventory. You should always stock up on items that sell fast. However, take caution and don't stock up on items that do not sell as fast.

WHAT'S YOUR PLAN TO CONTROL INVENTORY?

HOW TO CONTROL INVENTORY IN PRACTICAL STEPS

Small business owners have a lot of parts of the business to control, including controlling inventory for items you sell or equipment you use to operate your business.

WHAT TO DO WITH ITEMS THAT WILL NOT SELL

When you carry an excess of inventory that will not sell you have to have a plan to get rid of the inventory. Will your suppliers take your supplies back and ship you updated inventory? Will you donate the inventory to a local charity? Will you discount the products and have a sale? Will you bundle the items with other popular items that sell? Will you have a buy-one-get-one-free sale to get rid of the items?

YOU CAN DISCOUNT THE ITEM AND HAVE A SALE

Have you thought about having a sale and discounting products that do not sell at the full retail price? Always look at ways to sell overstocked items. Even if it's a piece of equipment you no longer use, you can sell it then use the money from the sale to buy more inventory or equipment.

YOU CAN BUNDLE THE ITEMS WITH OTHER POPULAR ITEMS

Do you have an item that is selling fast? If so, see if you can create a bundle package with an item that is not selling as fast as you would like. Shoppers like to buy added value items. You can bundle services too.

YOU CAN OFFER BUY ONE ITEM GET ONE FREE

Do you like buy one-get-one-free sales? Try it! Offer a service at buy-one-service-get-one-service free. Test the market and see how it works. This is a great way to get rid of items that are not selling.

WHEN TO REPLACE EQUIPMENT AND HOW OFTEN

You may have equipment to operate your business. Create a plan so you'll know how often you should replace equipment and know when it's time to buy new equipment.

I do this by using the equipment in my business until I can't use it anymore.

When it comes to overstocking on equipment, order only what you are going to need to effectively operate your business. Why

have extra equipment sitting in storage or a back room? And why have extra equipment saying, "use me."

Growing your business does not mean you have to get a lot more equipment to operate your business. Practice using what you have and worry less about what you don't have because as your business grows, you can upgrade your equipment if it no longer has use.

AVOID OVERSTOCKING SUPPLIES

Do not overstock supplies. Instead you may want to invest the extra cash you are spending on supplies such as printer ink.

TOMEKA PRESCOTT

Supplies to operate your business can be things such as:

- Ink
- Paper
- Tape
- Pens

I tend to buy supplies for my small business as needed and keep an inventory count of what I have in stock and the supplies that are not in stock. Being able to see everything on paper allows me to effectively reorder the supplies in a timely manner.

It may be helpful to control inventory by processing large orders weekly or monthly instead on a daily basis. This will cut down on shipping and freight charges, too. If it's not peak season for your business, you may want to avoid ordering in bulk if sales

are low, and be ready to stock up when sales rise again during peak season.

Learn effective strategies of controlling inventory. Draft a plan, implement your plan, and then make changes when needed.

USE WHAT YOU BUY

> *Use your resources over and over again, until you can't use them anymore. This may prevent you from overspending.*
>
> TOMEKA PRESCOTT

Your goal is to sell the items you buy, use the equipment you buy, and to use the supplies you buy, and not to overstock on these items and then not do anything with them. Once this concept has been learned, you're on your way to growing your business.

SUMMARY

Watching your bottom line and controlling inventory should be at the top of your to-do list. Continue to work on ways to strengthen your bottom line. Also, continue to control inventory the right way. Know that this takes hard work. You can do it!

IF YOU DO NOTHING ELSE AFTER READING THIS CHAPTER

Create a plan of how you will watch your bottom line and control your business inventory to be successful as a small business owner.

BOTTOM LINE:

Start out by writing down what you need to monitor.

Is it cash flow?

CONTROLLING INVENTORY:

Start out by making a list of your best selling products and services and making a list of the products and services that do not sell.

You can download an inventory worksheet summary at:

www.TomekaPrescott.com

Let's see what's in store in Chapter 11.

Chapter 11

HUMAN RESOURCES

Let's fuel the economy; let's light it up!
TOMEKA PRESCOTT

When I hear and read about people not being able to find jobs so they can provide for their families and themselves, my heart melts. I feel if we all work together as a community and as small business owners, we can create jobs to strengthen our economy.

When you think of human resources, what do you think about? Do you think about how and when you should hire employees? Do you think about what it takes to build a quality staff? Do you think about how you're going to manage a staff and operate your business at the same time? Do you think about learning how to

effectively manage your staff? Do you wonder if you have enough money to bring on a staff?

I have thought about all of these questions.

But since I know that people need jobs to provide for their families, I know that it's important to create jobs for people who live in a community. As a small business owner, I had to learn how to push forward to create jobs.

When I think about human resources, I think about how it is a part of my responsibility to create jobs as a small business owner. I think about how I can help fuel the economy.

TOMEKA PRESCOTT

I don't think it should be challenging for small business owners to create jobs. I believe creating jobs should be an easy task. I believe creating jobs should be something that all business owners do.

REBUILDING AN ECONOMY

When the economy is rebuilding I feel that everybody can help in the rebuilding process. No matter if you are rich or poor. No matter if you are in the middle class. No matter where you live on the map. No matter how many resources you have or don't have. I believe it's going to take you, as a small business owner, to have an unselfish regard towards others.

- It's going to take you, the small business owner, putting on your sneakers or flats, rolling up your sleeves, and mapping out plans to help build up your local

community. It's going to take you doing the best you can to get an education, because an education is so important. I worked really hard to earn my degrees because I knew this at a young age.

- It's going to take you, the small business owner, to throw away the excuses and get fired up to share your skills and knowledge with others to help fuel the economy. It's going to take working together with others to reach a common goal.

- It's going to take you, the small business owner, to know what's needed in your local economy, then help fill that need.

- Simply put, I want you to help people all that you can. I can keep going but I must stop here… on to learning about human resources, one department that I've grown to love.

WHAT I'VE LEARNED FROM MY DAD

Untying my daddy's shoes after a long day of hard work became a routine for me when I was a child. I even pulled off his socks. This was challenging to do as a kid. My dad wore the long tube socks; he would sometimes wear two pairs. They were white, not the ones with the two color lines if you remember those.

As I pulled the hardest I could, I would fall on the floor once I managed to take his socks off. I thought that was so much fun. Even though I would fall, I would always get back up. But there was one thing that I noticed while doing this for my dad. I noticed that…

MY DAD HAD A DAILY ROUTINE

My dad instilled his hard work ethic in me at a young age. I would see him wake up at 4 or 5 each morning to leave for work. Before he would leave, he would check on my siblings and me to make sure we were okay. He prepared breakfast for us so we would have a good start before going to school and even ironed our clothes before school. He would return home around 3:30 p.m. and do this same routine all over again. He did it for 20+ years until he retired.

Just like my dad did, I want you to get into a routine.

The routine you create can be to help create jobs for other people. How can you create jobs?

YOU HAVE THE POWER TO INSPIRE OTHERS TO WORK

Small business owners have the power to help inspire others to work. The power is *IN YOUR HANDS* to help build your local economy. It is going to take local communities working together to make our world a better place to live. I encourage you to consider how you'll plan to create jobs as a small business owner. I am creating jobs to help fuel the economy, and so can you!

ARE YOU HELPING TO CREATE JOBS FOR OTHER PEOPLE?

You may think you're not; however, if you are:

- Promoting other businesses' products and services.

- Networking through business partners to help grow their business.
- Sending referrals to small business owners.

You are helping to create jobs for others.

I commend you for doing this! It's good to network with others to help lift them up. You never know how much impact you may have in their lives. You also may never know how much you are helping them change the world for the good. As a small business owner, continue to work on creating jobs for others. It can be rewarding.

You know that creating jobs is in your hands as a small business owner.

WORKING AS A SMALL BUSINESS OWNER IS NOT LIKE WORKING A 9-5 JOB

We are not clocking in and out, as if we were working a 9-5 job because we are indeed small business owners. It's a business; it's your small business. Some people may think that if they only work 9-5 when trying to grow a business everything will work out. There is more to business.

I think differently. I think that while you can, you must put your all into working your business, even if it is before 9 a.m. and after 5 p.m.; you really have to put in those extra hours if you want to see growth.

Work your business as long as you can, and write your extra hours down on paper. You can call the extra hours you work, "growing" hours. I'm not saying overwork yourself though,

because when growing a business, you can start small and work yourself where you want to be.

- Remember that you can take as many breaks as you like.
- You don't have to overwork.
- You should always schedule in "me" time to kick back and relax.

WHAT IS LEARNING ABOUT HUMAN RESOURCES ABOUT?

What can you do to make strengthening our community a reality?

What can we do to put people to work?

TOMEKA PRESCOTT

This chapter is about the human resource department in your business. If you have any employees and/or business partners, you'll need to know how to train and motivate your employees to perform job tasks and deal with other people in the workplace.

In this chapter, you'll learn how to deal with other people in the workplace and you'll learn different strategies to motivate employees in the workplace.

Will you hire employees to help you grow your business?

WHY IS HIRING EMPLOYEES IMPORTANT?

Hiring employees shouldn't be a challenging task. As a small business owner, you may have no other choice but to hire employees to help operate your small business.

I've hired employees to help me operate and grow my small business.

Some small business owners have employees who help them and some don't hire employees to help them. We are going to look at practical steps for hiring and training employees.

BUILDING YOUR DREAM TEAM

When you grow your small business, you may have to bring on additional staff to help operate the business.

You are a smart worker, you are motivational, you are inspiring; however, what about your employees and/or helpers?

Are they like you too?

HIRING EMPLOYEES: WHAT ARE SOME THINGS YOU CAN LOOK FOR WHEN HIRING EMPLOYEES?

ARE THEY HELPERS?

You want to build a team of helpers, people who don't mind helping grow your business.

ARE THEY PASSIONATE ABOUT WORKING IN THE INDUSTRY?

When employees are passionate about working in the industry, you can tell and others can, too. Customers will tell you how passionate your employees are and will congratulate you for creating a team of passionate employees or helpers.

ARE THEY SMART WORKERS?

Can they help you make completing tasks easier to manage?

Can they streamline processes to make your business easier to operate?

Are they able to pull out their creativeness and relate it to the business?

DO THEY WANT TO HELP GROW YOUR BUSINESS?

What are they doing to help grow your business?

Are they referring your business to family members and friends?

Are they asking you how they can improve as an employee?

ARE THEY ASPIRING SMALL BUSINESS OWNERS TOO?

Would they like to operate their own business one day?

Do they have entrepreneurship characteristics?

Do they have small business owners' characteristics?

DO THEY LOVE HELPING OTHERS?

Do your employees love to help other people? Are they nice and kind to others? Are they friendly?

DO THEY HAVE A HEART TO HELP ALL? HOW MUCH DO THEY LOVE TO HELP OTHERS?

As a small business owner, you'll meet a lot of different types of people and so will your employees. It will be important to help people who are in need and to have a lot of love to help all.

DO THEY LOVE LEARNING SOMETHING NEW?

Make sure your employees love to learn because learning something new will most likely happen on a daily basis.

SOME MORE QUESTIONS YOU CAN THINK ABOUT ARE:

- Are they humble?
- Are they passionate about the company's mission and vision?
- Do they go the extra mile?
- Are they motivational?
- Are they inspiring?
- Are they HAPPY?

The employees who work at my small business fit in all of these categories and it's inspiring to

have the opportunity to work with them. They inspire me. I inspire them. We inspire each other. We have created an environment of inspiration.

TOMEKA PRESCOTT

TRAINING: WHAT TOOLS WILL YOU USE AND HOW WILL YOU TRAIN YOUR EMPLOYEES

Train leaders. Share your knowledge. Build a chain of leaders. We can sit down and continue to read about it or we can take action. I was born with skills to lead and have developed my leadership skills. I have a team and you can too.

TOMEKA PRESCOTT

While I knew training employees may be hard work that was okay because I learned all about hard work through my dad's hard work ethics.

Once you've hired your employees you'll need to train them to perform their job duties; you'll also need to create strategies to motivate your employees. How can you do this?

I am an educator so when I am training my employees I use teaching strategies and techniques. I train like I teach so I am reaching all learning styles such as visual and kinesthetic.

All training is on the job, hands-on; there is no meeting room, and there is no board room. Meetings take place on the floor and

happen when we have a question, or when we are planning our next project.

Training sessions are held throughout the day via real-life interaction with customers via smartphones, computers, and tablets. My small business is in the technology industry so I use technology gadgets to train employees.

During business meetings, we talk about how we can work together to create a plan for business growth. We talk about how we're going to fund and grow the projects that we've created to help make the world a better place and how we envision our projects getting bigger and bigger every year.

We've talked about what it takes to be #1 in our market.

We've talked about how we are going to use technology to help us streamline training.

We've talked about furthering education.

Training sessions and business meetings should be engaging so think of creative ways you can train your employees.

The question is...

Are you going to operate your business by yourself or are you going to hire employees to help you? This is an important question, however only you can answer it. Knowing when and who to hire to help you is very important. As a small business owner, I have a couple of employees who help me operate my business—and the rest of the help comes from outsourcing different parts of my business.

We will talk about outsourcing departments in Chapter 12, so hold on.

Sometimes you may have to have a side job or even a full-time job while you are growing your small business.

TOMEKA PRESCOTT

SUMMARY

Learn all you can about human resources. Be the one who rebuild the economy. Be the one who inspire others to work. You can build your dream team. Now, let's get started.

CREATE YOUR DREAM TEAM IF YOU DO NOTHING ELSE AFTER READING THIS CHAPTER

Create a list of the people who you envision to be on your "dream" team to help grow your small business.

Dream Team Employee

Dream Team Employee

Dream Team Employee

As I have mentioned earlier, I grew up working in a family business. Business success didn't happen overnight; it didn't happen in a year or two. The success strategies in this book have been used for the past 20 years to grow the business and will continue to be used to grow the business.

Who said that it doesn't take a long time grow a successful business? The journey may be long, but that's okay. I want you to have fun through the process. That's why it's important to celebrate success.

As you read the last couple of chapters of the book, take a break and reflect on the information you've learned so far. Continue to stay focused as we continue our journey together. You can be the future leader that you were created to be. As you continue to read, see yourself being that leader.

You can also review more resources at:

www.TomekaPrescott.com

Now let's turn to Chapter 12, where you'll learn all about outsourcing departments.

SECTION SIX

Looking Ahead

OUTSOURCE DEPARTMENTS

As you continue to grow your business, you may have to outsource departments to have extra helping hands.

TOMEKA PRESCOTT

In business, I don't see anything wrong with outsourcing departments when you feel that you have too many tasks to complete in one day, and you're not able to do everything all by yourself. It's good to share your workload with other people who are willing to help grow your small business. I do this, and it has made things so much easier.

I receive help and encouragement from people all over the world who live in places such as London, California, Florida, New York, Brazil, North Carolina, and Africa.

I can't forget about my local area, South Carolina. These people are so sweet to me! I love them all.

HOW AND WHEN TO OUTSOURCE DEPARTMENTS

Do you have to operate a small business all by yourself? I don't think so. This chapter is about knowing when and how to outsource departments.

In this chapter, you will explore strategies I've used to outsource departments.

So what is outsourcing? Outsourcing simply mean hiring other people or businesses to help you perform job tasks such as the payroll department in human resources. This is one department I have outsourced in my small business.

WHY IS OUTSOURCING IMPORTANT?

I am a teacher. I am not a singer, could possibly be a dancer if I worked at it—extra hard. I meant extra, extra, extra hard! You have to know what you can do in business to grow your business. If there is something you cannot do, ask for help.

TOMEKA PRESCOTT

Outsourcing departments is important because you may want to spend more time doing the job you specialize in as a small business owner. You may want to have more freedom to do other things you like, such as take a trip or go on vacation while your business is still open.

Allowing other people to help you can free up more of your time to spend with family members and friends—or work on that growth project you've always wanted to pursue. Since this book is loaded with a lot of growth project ideas, you may even want to set aside more time to tackle some of these or even create your own growth projects.

YOU CAN HELP OTHERS GROW THEIR BUSINESS

When you outsource departments, you help other small business owners or corporations grow their businesses, too, so they can help others as well. It's like a domino effect. There will be a lot of help being passed along, which is always a positive thing. I believe if you can help others—why not? Think about how you can link-up with other business owners.

OUTSOURCE IF IT'S THE RIGHT TIME

As a small business owner you may want to do it all; however, I don't think it's a bad idea to outsource departments if you need to—only if it's the right time. I've decided to outsource the payroll department in my small business because I wanted to have more time to spend interacting with customers and training employees.

I conducted research to see how I was going to get help in this area and then decided to go with the best option. This was a learning process for me, too. Thus far, everything is working well. I am now able to focus more on other parts of operating my small business.

THE RIGHT TIME TO OUTSOURCE DEPARTMENTS

You have to not only know when the time is right, but you also have to be ready, too. Continue to prepare yourself for business growth.

TOMEKA PRESCOTT

When you need the extra help to operate your business, you'll know when it's time to ask for help or simply outsource departments—it may be when you feel bogged down with so much to do, or when you may need a specialist to help you with a task or a growth project. It may be when you want to focus on your specialty, or focus more on customer service, and customer events.

OUTSOURCING IN PRACTICAL STEPS

Knowing when and how to outsource departments can help small business owners grow their business.

TOMEKA PRESCOTT

You can do this by creating a list of things you may need extra help with, then conduct some research to see who can help you and how much they will charge to help you. You don't have to rush the process of outsourcing tasks; as you grow your business you should be able to see where you need the additional help.

I used the Internet to conduct research and have talked with specialized agents with the company I have chosen to do business with (outsourced payroll department) to gather information about why this department should be outsourced and how it could benefit my small business.

PAYROLL DEPARTMENT

I don't specialize in payroll or human resources so I thought it would be a good start to get some help.

I contacted a local bank and asked them about the payroll services offered for small business owners. I was informed by the bank that I could outsource my payroll department to them so I can focus on the things I specialize in.

Getting set up with a local bank wasn't a long process. I immediately started the paperwork during my initial call.

Once I'd outsourced this department, I continued to monitor everything to ensure I'm keeping up with the up-to-date laws and regulations. I monitor this department throughout the week, and have linked up with a human resource company to help me stay up-to-date with the new payroll laws and regulations.

While I've outsourced payroll, I am the one who submits the payroll information and keep the records on file.

FREELANCERS

There are several places you can use on the Internet to outsource departments. If you have a task that needs to be completed, you can conduct an Internet search to find a freelancer to help you.

EVALUATE

Evaluate the departments that you've outsourced on a daily, weekly, or monthly basis to see if things are working out as planned. This is an important part when you decide to outsource departments. Just because you've made the decision to outsource a department, does not mean you should not monitor and evaluate other peoples' work.

Remember that you're the owner of your small business so you're going to be the one who knows what you really need to operate a successful business.

MONITOR

Even though I have outsourced a department and/or tasks, I still monitor and work in the department I have outsourced and I monitor the tasks. You don't have to be a micro manager; however, it's important to keep data and keep logs of what's happening with the tasks you've outsourced.

Now that you know more about outsourcing departments, create a list of areas where you believe you need extra hands.

Let's get started!

EXTRA HANDS

Extra hand 1

Extra hand 2

Extra hand 3

Extra hand 4

Extra hand 5

Now that you've created a list, are you going to be the extra hand or will you outsource departments? It's up to you; you're the small business owner. If you have already outsourced departments, what are these departments?

How does it benefit you to strengthen and grow your small business?

OUTSOURCING SOCIAL MEDIA MARKETING

The next task I will consider for outsourcing is social media marketing. I think this would be a great department to outsource, because it's now time to take social media marketing to the next level to grow my small business.

How do you outsource social media marketing?

Social media marketing can be outsourced through a company that offers social media services or through virtual assistants.

OUTSOURCING CUSTOMER ENGAGEMENT

A small business owner must have patience, an arena full of patience with helping customers. Don't worry if you are a small

business owner with little patience; you can improve in this area. Just keep reading this book. As you learn these strategies, then work on implementing these strategies, you will grow to become a better small business owner. If you find that you struggle with creating the customer engagement for your small business, that's okay.

I specialize in providing ways a small business can help improve customer engagement.

If you need help with creating a warm and friendly shopping environment for your customers, I have created a document for you to download at: www.TomekaPrescott.com

Once you've downloaded the document, you will have access to what I do to make my customers happy, and to make their shopping experience memorable. An experience that they love to get over, and over again.

To get started, here are a few tips to help you.

- **Create community events.**

  Your community is where you live, and holding events at your place of business in your community can benefit many people. Find out what you love and what your customers love, then create an event. These events can be online or at your physical store location. I have discussed this in detail in Chapter 4.

- **Provide alternate ways your customers can contact you via email or office phone.**

  Having multiple ways to be contacted is a good idea because you are giving your customers options. If they don't have time to pick up the phone and call, you have

opened lines of communication via other channels such as email.

- **Post answers to frequently asked questions on your social media pages for customers to read. For example, your store hours and phone number.**

  As a small business owner, you will have customers ask you the same questions over and over again, each and every day. Your goal is to make a list of frequently asked questions to post where they can be seen.

- **Let your customers know that you are experienced in your industry.**

  Share your credentials with your customers. If you are a college graduate, let your customers know. If you have 10 years of experience working in your industry, post it so the world can see.

  This will add value to your business, as well as build trust with your customers.

- **Be kind to your customers.**

  Have an open ear. Being kind will help you build valuable relationships.

Focus on making your customers happy; remember what I wrote about in Chapter 4. Customers are your best assets!

As a small business owner, while you think you may be good at performing a lot of different tasks, there are those tasks that need to be handled by other people who specialize.

Let's look at marketing for example.

Outsourcing Marketing

When you need help with finding new trends in a market, you can outsource that task to an expert. You can read about how I keep up with marketing trends at: www.TomekaPrescott.com

Let's look at why it may be important to have a plan to follow trends.

> *Know what trends you're going to follow; you don't have to follow them all. It's your choice.*
>
> Tomeka Prescott

It is important to keep up with market trends.

One trend I am seeing is the colorful bright products that are being manufactured and sold in different markets. I don't want to be left behind, so in my plan, I am creating a neon store theme and plan to be colorful and celebrate just like the other businesses. Your plan does not always have to be the new idea or invention, but I believe you should put your own touch of creativity to whatever you are doing.

I am upgrading my red and white gift cards to neon colors like bright yellow, lime green, and hot pink.

I am upgrading my retail shopping bags to colors like bright blue, orange, and yellow.

I am upgrading my inventory by purchasing these popping bright color products to sell in my store.

If you're my customer and you are reading this—get ready for the new products. Get ready for a splash of eye-catching color products.

Get ready for a change!

Do you see where I am going? There is a trend going on in the market and I believe it's a good one, so I'm going to follow and implement this trend. As a small business owner, it's up to you to keep up with what's going on in your market and it's up to you to implement the ideas in your small business. It's up to you to create a budget and a plan when you tackle growth projects like this one.

As you continue to grow your business, you will gain experience and knowledge about when and not to follow market trends. The location of your business is very important when looking at what trends you should follow. While a trend may be successful in New York City, it may not work in another state. I've seen large retailers or businesses that have sold the same products in one state and have been successful; however, the same items in another state were not successful. Knowing how to analyze a market is very important.

How do you outsource market trending?

Market trending can be outsourced through a company that offers marketing trending services or through virtual assistants.

Should I outsource? Or should I complete the task myself? This is something good to think about. Don't rush this step.

TOMEKA PRESCOTT

One more benefit of outsourcing tasks and departments is that it may prevent burnouts. I don't think anyone likes burnouts. Chapter 1 is where I've told you about a burnout that I had.

SUMMARY

Know how and when to outsource departments. You don't have to do everything all by yourself. Helpers can help you. Now, let's get started. You can do it!

THINK ABOUT DEPARTMENTS YOU CAN OUTSOURCE IF YOU DO NOTHING ELSE AFTER READING THIS CHAPTER

You can create a list of departments you may want to think about outsourcing now or in the future.

Department 1

Department 2

Department 3

Department 4

Department 5

❖

I want to thank you for reading Chapter 12 of this book.

If this is the chapter you've started to read first I want you to read the other chapters as well because there is a lot of valuable information in each chapter.

Let's move on to Chapter 13 where you'll learn how to inspire others through your mission and vision.

SECTION SEVEN

End Notes

Be an angel. Be a star. You can go far, but remain true to who you are.

TOMEKA PRESCOTT

Notes:

STAY TRUE TO WHO YOU ARE AND YOUR OWN BUSINESS MISSION BUT REMAIN OPEN TO WHAT MIGHT HAPPEN AND WHO YOU MIGHT INSPIRE BY CARRYING OUT YOUR VISION

Who am I? I am human. My name is Tomeka Prescott. I am a woman born and raised in the South. I was born to be a TEACHER. Therefore, I am shining my light by touching the world with my knowledge and love. I am an author. A talent that was embedded in me all along and pulled out through implementation and with the help of my valued friends.

I am a small business owner here to help you grow your small business.

I AM AN INTROVERT WITH FEW EXTROVERT QUALITIES

Being an introvert, I get ENERGY from things like writing this book. Being able to express myself through writing is exciting! However, having group conversations, or having a lot of eyeballs looking at me takes all of my energy. It eats it up, but I know that I can't let this stop me from doing what I was called to do. Instead, I take small steps to strengthen my extrovert qualities.

I do this through:

- Public Speaking Engagements
- Beauty Pageants
- Managing my small business on a day-to-day basis.

MY LOVE FOR LEARNING

In preschool, I found out that I really loved learning. My mom would tell me that I never wanted to miss a day of school. Striving for perfect attendance each school year was my goal; I would even go to school when I was sick. While in classes I wouldn't say much because I was a shy student. I was blessed to have a great mom to help me develop my teaching skills at a young age and was blessed to have teachers who were able to help me in overcoming my shyness in class. I was also blessed to have fantastic grade school teachers who were able to adapt to my learning style to help push me forward in each grade level.

I remember who you all are; and I am thankful to have had you as teachers. I value all of my teachers. Also, I was blessed to have

my parents help me prepare for my first college teaching position.

MY LOVE FOR TEACHING

Since I was a little girl I loved to teach. It wasn't until I got older that I realized that I was born to teach.

TOMEKA PRESCOTT

While I knew I loved school and anything to do with teaching and learning, I would have never known that I would graduate college at the age of 21 and graduate school at the age of 23. Also, become a college professor at the age of 26, operate and manage a retail store, teach over 40 business courses, author 3 business college tests that were published to help students worldwide learn about business, write my first book, teach an Introduction to Psychology class, and teach my first Introduction to Business college course to international students who live in Malawi, Africa, and Jordan by the age of 30. I know now that I was born to teach.

I am humbled.

YOU HAVE TO HAVE CONFIDENCE

I want you to rock your market. Give it a little shake.

TOMEKA PRESCOTT

I POUR OUT MY ALL TO MY STUDENTS

While I know that everyone has unique learning skills, I want to be able to help push my students forward, no matter what level they are on. I am able to adapt to each learner. That's my teaching philosophy. That's how I teach.

TOMEKA PRESCOTT

Yes, confidence is the key!

You must have confidence!

Having confidence in yourself can take you further than you could ever imagine. If there is a goal that you want to accomplish in life- like a goal to create a business plan when you are already in business—you can do it! Teaching my first college class at the age of 26 years old was a dream come true, but I had to have the confidence to know that I could get the job done. My students ranged from the age of 19 to 60+. At first I thought, how I am going to control this class. Guess what? I thought and I thought, but this did not help much. I have worked so hard to gain the knowledge so that I could teach but when I got the opportunity to show the world my skills, I was happy, but scared all at the same time. I was scared, really, I was! I knew that I could get the job done and teaching was my passion, but where did my confidence go? Or did I really have confidence? Yes, it was there, but I had to find it. My parents told me that I could do this, and my friends told me that I could do it, but I had to tell myself that I know I can do this—and that's what I did.

I have been teaching college courses online since 2009, and absolutely love it. I was successful through planning. When I stay true to who I am I can see that…

DREAMS COME TRUE

What I have learned is that dreams really come true through hard work and love, and to never give up on the things you want to accomplish in life. I have also learned that it is really important to share your knowledge with others because there is a reason why you have the talent to do the things you do. Whether it's growing your business, writing books, dancing, singing, and much more.

I HAD A DREAM

In my dream I was in Africa sitting in a classroom full of smart students eager to learn. Well, this dream is being turned into reality. On May, 5th of 2014 (the same day I graduated from college in 2001) I received my first class of international students from Malawi, Kenya, and Jordan, who will have an opportunity to earn college credit for an Introduction to Business course. I am prepping; I am getting ready.

My eyes were filled with joyful tears when I found out that I would teach Introduction to Business to international students. Being able to touch people throughout the world with my business knowledge and love is a dream come true. I'm thankful to be surrounded by a group of professor colleagues who have helped me grow in so many ways.

Prof. Prescott is on her way to Africa and Jordan, not physically, but remotely. I will teach this class online. I don't have to be there physically to shine my light. I can do this through writing.

This is why I love to teach online! I'm humbled to have this experience and I want you to stay humbled, so you don't overlook your success. Success can be something big or small; it can mean something different to all.

As a small business owner, tell the world what you do because you'll never know who you may inspire one day.

I am here to tell you to grow where you are. Don't wait until you have received a grant that you have applied for. Don't wait for someone to write a grant for you. Don't wait until you relocate where you want to be. Don't wait until after your friends and colleagues have made the choice to grow.

I Teach Business, Ethics, And Communication Courses

I want to let you know that…

Good teachers who love what they do and who love all will help create an environment of learners who are eager to do their best. No matter where the learners come from or what learning level they are on, it would not matter because the learners will know that good teachers will catch them so they won't have the fear of failure at learning when they can't see the whole staircase.

When learners can't see the whole staircase, they may have the fear of failure, but I am here to catch them before they fall.

I am here to meet them on their level to help push them forward.

> **One child, one teacher, one pen**
> **and one book can change the world.**
>
> MALALA YOUSAFZAI

As I have indicated in Chapter 1, life goes on and business works the same way. Some days you may generate a lot of income, and some days you may sell nothing. This is why planning and building that cushion that I discussed in the Watching Your Bottom Line chapter is important in business.

I WANT TO LEAVE YOU WITH THESE FOUR QUOTES:

If we all did the things we are capable of doing, we would literally astound ourselves.

THOMAS EDISON

Focus on building a global community. You can go global. You can help people no matter where they live on the map.

Tomeka Prescott

Continue to apply each lesson you've learned to your small business. This really makes learning fun and exciting.

TOMEKA PRESCOTT

Don't look back—keep pushing forward and never give up on seeing your vision in life.

TOMEKA PRESCOTT

THIS IS WHAT I WANT YOU TO DO

SHINE BRIGHT!

How can small business owners shine bright?

Such as small business owners who may not have the buying power as larger businesses. Small business owners who may sometimes find it hard to earn a profit. Small business owners who work hard day in and day out to ensure they are keeping their customers happy.

I thought and thought, and realized that as a small business owner, the power is *In Your Hands* whether or not you want to grow your small business, whether you want to be successful, and how far you want to go. It's *In Your Hands* how many people you plan to help and what kind of legacy you plan to leave. It's *In Your Hands* what kind of work you produce and what kind of quality products and services you offer in your small business to sell to your customers. But you have to believe it—it's all *In Your Hands*. Shine Bright!

IN YOUR HANDS

STAY FOCUSED

Plenty of times while writing this book I had to refer back to Chapter 1, the chapter about staying focused.

The information in Chapter 1 helped me stay focused on completing this book. There were plenty of distractions, but I had to keep moving.

THIS IS WHAT I WANT YOU TO REMEMBER

Remember that it's not about how much education you have under your belt; it's not about boasting about the things you have. It's about how you can meet others on their level to give them a lift, whether it's a family member, friend, customer, a business partner, colleague, supplier, and employee. Serving others is important. You can start where you live. My eyes are wide open, so I want to see what you are doing to help uplift others. I want to see your business growth.

It does not matter what level you are on, I am here to help push you forward; and no it's not like a push in the back. I remember in grade school at recess some kids thought it was fun to push their friends from behind, say you're it, then run very fast the other way. Do you remember that? Well, I am going to walk and grow with you, too. As you grow your small business, walk in love because you may never know who you may inspire.

The journey of business growth should not be one that you go on by yourself.

Let's take the first step together.

❖

Be the one who grows your community in a way that is far beyond what you could have ever imagined. Be the one who takes the lead. Be the one who is sweet like cupcakes to others.

TOMEKA PRESCOTT

I WANT TO SIGN OFF WITH THIS...

This is what I had for you. I had to release this book. Now, I want you to take your business to the next level. SHAKE UP YOUR MARKET, WAKE IT UP! Go on and live out your dreams.

I am proud of you!

Hugs,

Tomeka Prescott

www.TomekaPrescott.com

Tomeka

Acknowledgement

Dear God: I love You! I will walk in Your will.

To Dad (Herbert) and Mom (Mary): You have helped me put this book *IN YOUR HANDS*. I am blessed to have you as parents. I love you!

To my siblings (Larry, Travis, Felisha, and Tevin): You have bright and prosperous futures ahead. I love you!

To my half-brother (Michael): Thank you so much for your encouraging words. I love you!

To my sisters- in-law, brother-in-law, nieces, and nephews. I love you.

To my family members: Thank you for your support! Hugs!

To Damon: It is a blessing I have met you. Thank you so much for your help. You are inspirational and a great role model.

To Cathy Presland: This was a huge book project. You were with me throughout the entire process. I am thankful to have met you! You are a great leader and mentor.

To my friends: Thank you for your support!

To Kimyarda Abraham (hair stylist): Thank you for your encouraging words! You are kind!

To Michelle Booth (Book formatter): Thank you! : -)

To Leslie Bowman (Editor): Thank you! : -)

http://www.profbowman.com/EDITING.html

To www.caroline-king.com (Cover designer): Thank you!

To Eliza Gordner, J.D.: Thank you! I appreciate your help.

To the photographer (Photo by Johnathan Carter) and (Stylist hair/Makeup by Heather Carter). Thank you! The photo shoot was amazing!

To my professor colleagues: You walk with me to help turn my dreams into reality. I am humbled. The list is long. You know who you are. Thank you!

To Patrice Tubbs MBA, MA: Thank you! You are a great leader!

To Antionette Dee Richardson MAHR, MAHRDV,

MAOM: Thank you! You are the best!

To my teachers: Thank you for the learning experience each one of you have created.

To my students: I enjoy teaching you. Continue to push forward.

To my customers: Thank you! You are truly valued! I am grateful you allow me to serve you.

To the promotion team: Thank you!

To everyone who I have met in life I want to say, "thank you"!

Connect. Share. Serve.

www.TomekaPrescott.com

Email:tprescottins@aol.com